C000157594

Bramcote School

The First 100 Years

Bramcote School
The First 100 Years

Pip Land

The Pentland Press Limited
Edinburgh · Cambridge · Durham

© Bramcote School 1993

First published in 1993 by
The Pentland Press Ltd.
1 Hutton Close
South Church
Bishop Auckland
Durham

All rights reserved.
Unauthorised duplication
contravenes existing laws.

ISBN 1 85821 068 2

Typeset by Elite Typesetting Techniques, Southampton.
Printed and bound by BPCC Wheatons Ltd.

CONTENTS

ACKNOWLEDGEMENTS

This book would not have been possible without the enthusiastic and practical support of the staff at Bramcote School, especially John and Mary Gerrard, Peter Wilkinson, Richard Lytle and James Lundie. I am particularly grateful to the Gerrards for their warm hospitality and to the Toads for making my seven-year-old son so welcome. Living in at the school on occasions helped me to experience the reality of Bramcote today as well as keep up with a tough deadline. Lunchtimes proved a special experience – both for the good food and because the boys' questions made me aware of issues which I might well have otherwise missed.

And my special thanks to Richard Clive – without whom the true beauty of the old photographs (1900–1945) would not have been so apparent. Thanks also to Paul Norris for letting me repeatedly raid his up-to-date and excellent photographic records. Most of the photographs for the 1980s and 1990s were taken by him.

I very much appreciate how many people were willing to share with us unique family treasures. With thanks for the following illustrations to: Rev. Sir J. Alleyne Bt (7, 8 & 9); Canon G. Markham (34, letters pp. 32–33 & 38); Peter Thelwell (48); R. Cairns-Terry (51, 52 & 53), Mr. C. Gillam (re.63); Richard Wilkinson (64); William Sager (76); Colin McGarrigle (81); Mrs C. Hornby (89); Charles Moubray (letters pp.98–99); and to Gervase Markham jnr for his letter (p. 156). Richard Clive supplied us with no. 150 and John Fuller-Sessions with nos. 99, 100, and 116. Photographs originally sent to The Bramcotian were no. 1 (from Lady Chiesman) and no. 13 (from the Gardner-Smith family). George Bagshawe gave an album of photographs to the school many years ago, and from that illustration no. 12 was reproduced. Our thanks to Stephen Hollins-Gibson for the reproduction of no. 83 and to his wife, Poppy, for photograph no. 84. Illustration no.139 was reproduced by courtesy of the *Yorkshire Post*; and the following by courtesy of the *Scarborough Evening News* – 84, 85, 88, 134, 138, 139, and 147. We are grateful to Peter Robson for allowing us to copy information and an illustration from his book *The Fishing Robsons* (p14–15). James Lundie produced the computerised picture on page 158 using the school's new computer and desk top publishing facility. This is a book of reminiscences and it is not possible here to list all those who wrote in such fascinating letters or set aside their time to be interviewed, but they are acknowledged in the text. I am only sad I did not have more time to spend on research and regret I couldn't visit more Old Boys. My apologies to all those I missed! I am grateful to John Cundall for checking my draft copies. The information about Geoffrey Vickers VC was researched and supplied by Val Foster; and the details about the careers of Maurice Platnauer and John Humphrey were provided by Martin Dreyer.

John Walker gave the impetus for this book to become a reality this year, but I am especially indebted to Peter Wilkinson for his assistance with research, proof reading and inspiration.

P.L.

LIST OF ILLUSTRATIONS

INTRODUCTION

He was a shadowy figure in their history – the man who founded Bramcote School, Scarborough in 1893. Samuel Servington Savery planned to start the school with just one boy – Frederick Milner Spencer. In fact, he was able to begin the Michaelmas Term of 1893 with three boys. By September 1909 214 boys had studied at the school. Nine of these had gained scholarships to Public Schools and ten obtained naval cadetships. Others had passed the Common Entrance Examination to such schools as Harrow, Rugby, Uppingham, Repton and Oundle. The first scholarship was that of Maurice Platnauer in 1901 to Shrewsbury.

Samuel Savery retired from the school in 1911 and later went into politics. He won Holderness (by Hornsea) for the Conservatives in 1923 and served as their MP until shortly before his death in 1938. He was knighted in 1937 in the first Honours List of King George VI.

But the man who moulded Bramcote into one of the top two preparatory schools in the North, excelling in the classics and sports, and whose name became synonymous with it, was Richard Pidcock. Richard Pidcock and Douglas Slater were invited by Savery to join him as headmasters in 1909. Slater and Pidcock, as joint headmasters, began the system of each having pastoral and academic responsibility for half of the school. Slater, however, left in 1925. Pidcock was the sole headmaster for five years, until one of the masters at the school, Oswald Cooper, joined him in the partnership. The position of headmaster at that time was obtained by buying into the business. Christian names, for masters or boys, were rarely used in those early decades and Pidcock was usually referred to by his surname, initials or as 'Pidder'.

The new partnership lasted for 15 years with the school divided into Pidcock's and Cooper's boys. Pidcock retired immediately after the Second World War. At that time another master, Frank Hamerton, took a minor share in the partnership and in the early 1950s Oswald Cooper planned that two others, Jim Hornby and Sandy Stow, would also join them. After some years of deliberations, and with Stow's departure, the school eventually became an educational Charitable Trust in 1957 with Oswald Cooper as Chairman of the Board, a position he retained until 1970.

Under this new arrangement Jim Hornby and Frank Hamerton took over the joint headmastership. Jim Hornby fulfilled a pivotal role in the school's history. Through his connections with the Incorporated Association of Preparatory Schools, of which he became Chairman in 1966, he was keenly aware of the changes which were taking place within education. Until then classics and maths had dominated the Common Entrance Examinations but the need to change the curriculum was becoming apparent. It was through Jim Hornby that Bramcote was one of the pioneers among independent schools as regards teaching science.

The school came into an era of adventure and experimentation in the 1970s under Colin McGarrigle and John Fuller-Sessions, with boys and staff putting forward ideas which often went on to shape the school as it is today. As corporal punishment was phased out (beginning in the 1970s) new methods of discipline had to be formulated between the masters and the boys and John and Marion Fuller-Sessions were especially involved in this after Colin McGarrigle left in 1983. With them in this evolving process was a new assistant headmaster, John Gerrard, and his wife Mary. John Fuller-Sessions retired from the headmastership in 1990 and John Gerrard continued alone for over two years until he was joined by John Walker, and his wife Janie.

1. Samuel Servington Savery at the entrance to the school with some of his boys, c. 1895.

CHAPTER 1

A Firm Foundation
1893–1919

Savery probably never fitted the mould of a preparatory school headmaster –
Lumley Dodsworth who was one of his boys and became his friend in adulthood,
described him as a lovable and gentle personality. Another close friend, Lady
Chiesman, said he was a nice amusing little man and a great character and added:
'He was very outgoing and very charming. He loved teaching and was very
committed to the boys of his school.'

The son of Rev. George Savery of Oxford, he was educated at Kingswood,
Bath and Christ Church, Oxford, where he had a distinguished career and gained
his MA. He was a master at Summer Fields, the famous Oxford preparatory
school, from 1886 until 1888 when his brother, George Mearns Savery, was the
headmaster of what was then Harrogate College for Boys. In 1893 George Savery
opened Harrogate Ladies' College and the first headmistress was Miss Field-Hall.
In *Harrogate College 1893-1973* the author, Dorothy Hewlett, stated: 'Miss
Field-Hall was evidently greatly liked by her girls and much regret was expressed
when she gave up the headship and sought another post in 1898.'

Savery was about 32 years old when he founded Bramcote School. The first
entries in the Bramcote School Register, in meticulous copperplate writing, were
most likely written by his sister, Edith Savery. This handwriting continued until
Slater took over as joint headmaster in 1909.

In the notes he gave the school in 1937
(and written in the School Register
by Pidcock) Savery stated:

'I began my negotiations with only
one boy in view – Spencer. Just before
I opened, Spinks was entered. Three
weeks after term began, Cooper
joined. The school was named Bramcote after our home in the Banbury
Road, Oxford, of which my sister and
I were very fond. There is a village
near Nottingham called
Bramcote. Many people
thought that we had
associations with
that place. The
first Nottingham
parents told me

2. Samuel Servington Savery.

that it was the name which attracted them, and subsequently we had a very good Nottingham connection: the three brothers Hardy, two or three Parrs, Spendlove, Vickers our VC, and Sir Kenneth McCraith etc.'

In the 1910 school photograph there were 58 boys grouped around Savery, Pidcock and Slater. By the time Savery retired in April 1911 233 pupils had been registered since the school's inception. Sadly, 27 of these were to die in the First World War as did two of the masters who had been with Savery. The first clear mention of any additional teaching staff was recorded in 1897 (C.J. Greenwood). In 1898 the members of staff were J.D. Gould and Wright. Gould left after 24 terms to 'conduct a prep school at Westgate' by which time there were four members of staff, including one woman.

Little is known about what happened to many of the boys in the first two decades of the school's life. In 1898 it was recorded that Cecil Hudson had gone on to Brighton College; Charles White to Bedford County School and that Colin Reynolds had joined his brother, Seetham, at Wakefield Grammar School. Those gaining admittance to Public Schools included Alick Byass to Malvern College, and Clifford Wilson to The Leys in Cambridge.

Maurice Platnauer from York entered the school in the summer term of 1898 and by Easter of 1901 had almost overtaken George Savery Jessup, the fourth boy to enter the school (in 1894). Jessup left that Easter to join the York City and County Bank. Platnauer, the next term, made Bramcote history by becoming the first to win a scholarship – to Shrewsbury. He later took a double first at New College, Oxford and served in France during World War One before returning to his teaching post at Winchester.

Savery had brought the competitive form system from Summer Fields. This meant that a bright boy like Platnauer rapidly rose through the school whereas someone like Jessup might remain in the same form for several years until he finally made it to the top and could move up. Canon Gervase Markham (1921-24) commented:

'The whole system of prep school is that you go up as fast as you can. You go up among your peers and you compete to get on.' This did not change until the 1950s, but the aims of the school are still the same: to prepare boys for the Public Schools of their parents' choice.

With boys entering Public Schools like Winchester, Radley, Rugby, Uppingham, Haileybury, Harrow and Shrewsbury a pattern was taking shape that would be followed for the next 100 years. Savery's next scholarship boy was Percival Gardner-Smith in the summer of 1902 and two years later 'Jack' Alleyne was the first to gain a naval cadetship.

Savery probably modelled much of Bramcote on Summer Fields, the graces such as said before meat and after meat each lunchtime. At 91 years of age George Bagshawe (1910-1915) can still recite these. Savery also turned to Summer Fields when looking for someone to succeed him. Pidcock wrote in the School Register later:

'During 1909 R.D. Slater and R.G. Pidcock, both assistant masters at Summer Fields, Oxford joined Mr Savery. Slater came up in May 1909 as at that time it was expected that Mr Savery would be married in June, and Pidcock followed in September, from which date the triple partnership began.' The school was privately owned by Savery and his two new partners had to purchase their share of it – and eventually buy him out. The joint headmastership was to become an enduring feature of Bramcote. Savery's plans came to nothing, however, as Lady Chiesman recounted:

'He was going to marry the mother of some of the boys at the school but the boys didn't approve – so he remained a bachelor.' In his later years Savery was to quip: 'Marriage is not a word – it is a sentence.'

Pidcock and Slater inherited from him one of the most faithful masters in Bramcote's history – Walter Hemming (a cockney, according to Hugh Tapper) who joined in the Michaelmas Term of 1904 and retired with Pidcock in November 1945. 'Hemming was the one everyone liked,' commented Bagshawe. 'He was the maths master. We had maths prep every Saturday night.'

Like Savery, Pidcock and Slater were also Oxford graduates. But the triple partnership proved unworkable. Oswald Cooper (headmaster 1930-57) wrote many years later:

'Savery had very successfully launched the school, but he was somewhat old-fashioned in his ideas and methods; among other peculiarities he would allow no matches with other schools as he thought they engendered ill-feeling. Many changes now took place [when Slater and Pidcock arrived]. It is doubtful if there was one single point on which Slater and Pidcock agreed with Savery about the running of the school and Savery retired in 1911. Under Slater and Pidcock Bramcote was run on more orthodox lines.'

Savery and his sister moved to Harrogate where he remained closely connected with Harrogate Ladies' College, serving on their committee for many years, following the death of his brother in 1906. Edith Savery died during the First World War. The doctor who cared for her was Lady Chiesman's father. It was Savery, in the role of adoptive father, who introduced her to many of his Society friends when he was an MP and gave the address at her wedding. Lady Chiesman remembered him as being very good at relating to children and he was remembered with affection by those who wrote down their memories of him later. One of these was Rev. P. Gardner-Smith, who had become Dean of Jesus College, Cambridge 1922-56, a Fellow there from 1923-85 and President from 1948-58. He died in 1985 but three years earlier had written:

Savery was a remarkable man, an Oxford graduate, a most capable organiser, pleasant and genial, and popular with the boys although they had reason to recognise the 'Dr Grimstone' side of his character. He was a 'good disciplinarian'. What surprised me in later years was, that to teach those 30 boys there was the headmaster and four assistant masters, all Oxford or Cambridge men. He was greatly helped by his sister who managed domestic affairs and nursed the boys who were ill. What the assistant masters thought of him I should not know, but at least they stayed on their somewhat meagre stipends.

Life was fairly austere: Scarborough is a cold place in winter and spring, and the small coal fires in the big rooms failed to keep us warm. The bedrooms were unheated. Personally I suffered much from chilblains. We had our dramatic entertainments. Savery was a fine actor, and he did his best with the boys, particularly insisting that every word should be audible at the back of the room. Good training for a future clergyman and lecturer. I won a scholarship to Sherborne. I was not there long. My father did not like the school as it was then, and he could not afford it, so I went to Wakefield Grammar School instead – a school of very high academic reputation.

Lumley Dodsworth spent seven years at Bramcote from 1897. He wrote his notes for the school in 1939:

We used to have compulsory boxing for the whole school every Wednesday in the Michaelmas Terms in the gym (not the same as the present one) – under a Sergeant from the Barracks. I recollect taking part in more than one gory fight. In the summer we went twice a week to the swimming baths at the *Aquarium* – and on fine summer mornings Mr Savery took volunteers to bathe in the sea before breakfast. Push-bike races, fast and slow, were part of the Sports Day programme.

Mr Holliday, who afterwards became an Instructor-Captain in the Royal Navy (and had married Savery's niece), looked after the mathematical side with great ability. Every Wednesday night, instead of the usual prep, we were set a paper of 24 simple arithmetic questions and were given an hour in which to do them. Feeble performer though I was, I always looked forward to these tests of speed and accuracy, and the solitary occasion on which I notched 100 per cent was a great day for me. A number of boys passed into the Royal Navy from Bramcote, and much of their success was due to the way in which Mr Holliday prepared them for the important mathematical papers.

Mr Savery took little part in the actual teaching, but he was wont from time to time to pay devastating visits to form rooms and woe betide any malefactor who happened at the moment to be 'standing out'! It was certainly not easy to idle with impunity at Bramcote in my time.

Miss Savery, to whom much of Bramcote's early success was due, was a strong personality. She was a disciplinarian like her brother, but if a boy was homesick or ill she was kindness itself, and was on the whole loved by the boys.

One of the happiest recollections of the Bramcote of my time is the whole-day picnics. We used to have one of these at the start of the Michaelmas Term and another towards the end of the Easter Term and always two, at least, in the Summer Term. We also used to go to some strawberry gardens at Ayton once in the Summer Term, where each boy was regaled with as many strawberries as he could manage. I do not recall any ill effects.

Another happy memory is the way in which Miss Savery read to us on wet half holidays and at other times, while Mr Savery always read on Sunday night after Prayers. He was a magnificent reader, and I shall never forget the thrills of *Lot 241* and *Dr Jekyll and Mr Hyde*. It is only fair to say the younger boys were packed off to bed, though even for the elder ones it may be thought that these works were scarcely an incentive to a reposeful night! On half holidays Miss Savery turned shopkeeper and retailed chocolate slabs and bars to the boys. She did a thriving trade.

In my time there was a rage for a game called 'Paper Cricket'. A piece of paper was ruled into squares and the squares covered with the numbers one to six and also the words 'caught', 'bowled', 'lbw' etc. The player then shut his eyes and dabbed with his pencil on the board. Most thrilling matches were fought out, but somehow Yorkshire always won.

I remember Mr Leng, one of the parents, driving on to the playing field in the first motor car I ever saw. Amid great excitement he gave the boys rides round the ground. It was a red-letter day. Another notable day of a very different sort was the occasion of a terrific storm at Scarborough when there were nine ships wrecked on the coast between Cayton Bay and the Castle Hill. The whole school went down to the harbour, and I shall never forget the spectacle of a trawler in imminent peril of being dashed against the harbour wall and thanks to brilliant handling just saving itself. It was a thrilling scene. How we all cheered when the good ship was saved!

There were no 'leave-out' Sundays in my day. Boys were allowed to go out with their parents either on half-holidays or Sundays, but in pre-motoring days visits from parents were rare. Scarborough boys, like myself, were more fortunate – we were allowed to go home after Church until 6 p.m. every alternate Sunday.

3 & 4. Off for a picnic with Savery in 1910.

5. *Savery out with some of the boys c. 1908.*

6. *Henry Bolckow, Ronald Atkinson and Stanley Carr in 1909.*

'Guy Fawkes Day was commemorated wholeheartedly,' wrote Dodsworth. 'The fireworks were let off in the playing field. The boys were all provided with torches with wooden handles which burned for a good half-hour, and were very useful for lighting fireworks at a safe distance. Boys were not allowed to receive fireworks from home, but were allowed to buy them at school. A huge stall was set up in the gym and boys' expenditure varied with their age. In those days quite a good show could be made for 2s 6d. Rockets were taboo.'

Jack Alleyne, son of Sir John Alleyne Bt., was at Bramcote at the same time as Dodsworth. He was the first to get a naval cadetship from Bramcote, his being to the *Britannia* Royal Naval College in Dartmouth in 1904 when he was just 15 years old.

My dear Kathleen

Grandage one of the boys has got an 18/- box of fire-works and he has got two things the shape of a shell and it says on them, to be put twenty yards from any building and light the touch paper and stand clear immediately so I should think it will be a pretty big explosion, it's brown and done round with string it is a sort thing like this and about this size and there just a bit of paper like that at the top so it doesn't give you much time to get away. With love to all. Your affec brother Jack.

7. One of the letters Jack Alleyne wrote to his sister Kathleen while he was at Bramcote.

In May 1904 Savery wrote to Jack's father:

My dear Sir John Alleyne,

I have recently returned from a holiday in the Channel Islands, and I have found your very kind letter of congratulations awaiting me. I am very much obliged for your appreciation of our efforts with Jack. I am truly delighted that the result has proved as creditable to the dear boy, and so gratifying to his family circle. It would be difficult for me to exaggerate the joy and pleasure I have always felt in numbering him among my pupils. Throughout his long career here, he has shown himself to be possessed of such upright, steadfast, loyal and affectionate qualities, that I have regarded it as a privilege to have my share in the work of his training and development. When so much of a boy's destiny, as in this case, depends on the result of his studies, the onus of responsibility is very great and cannot fail to cause me some anxiety – but Jack has made the burden as light as possible for me, by his unwavering application, by his keenness, and by his cheerful trust and obedience. While he is to be congratulated on entering the *Britannia* as young and at his first attempt I feel that the Service is also fortunate in gaining such an admirable and promising recruit. I had the great pleasure of spending last Sunday at North Wootton, where I was able to see Jack arrayed in his uniform with his blushing honours full upon him! My thoughts have been very much with him today as he speeds West to join his ship. I know he will be happy in the life he has chosen and I am confident that, if he is spared, he will prove an increasing source of pride and comfort to you all.

With many thanks to you for writing so kindly to me.

Yours sincerely

Servington Savery.

One summer Jack wrote to his sister: 'On Wednesday we went for a pic-nick [sic]; we walked to Cayton Station and went by train to Filey and had dinner there in a sort of shop place and we were allowed to spend sixpence each but we only spent threepence because we thought we could spend another threepence afterwards but we could not but it did not matter much; after dinner we walked to Hunmanby and trained back to Scarborough, so all the work we did was half an hour in evening for our post-cards.'

8. Top right: Jack Alleyne carrying his bat out for his first match at Bramcote.
9. Insert: Jack, the schoolboy.
10. Bottom right: The boys at Cayton Bay around 1908.
11. Over: Sidney Davies attended Bramcote from 1899 until 1903 when he left for Harrogate College. In his report cards for each term notes were written about what he had covered in the following subjects: 'Latin, French, Scripture, Arithmetic, Algebra, Euclid, History, Greek, Geography, Repetition and Trigonometry.' Davies' total bill for the Easter Term 1902 was £39.14s.

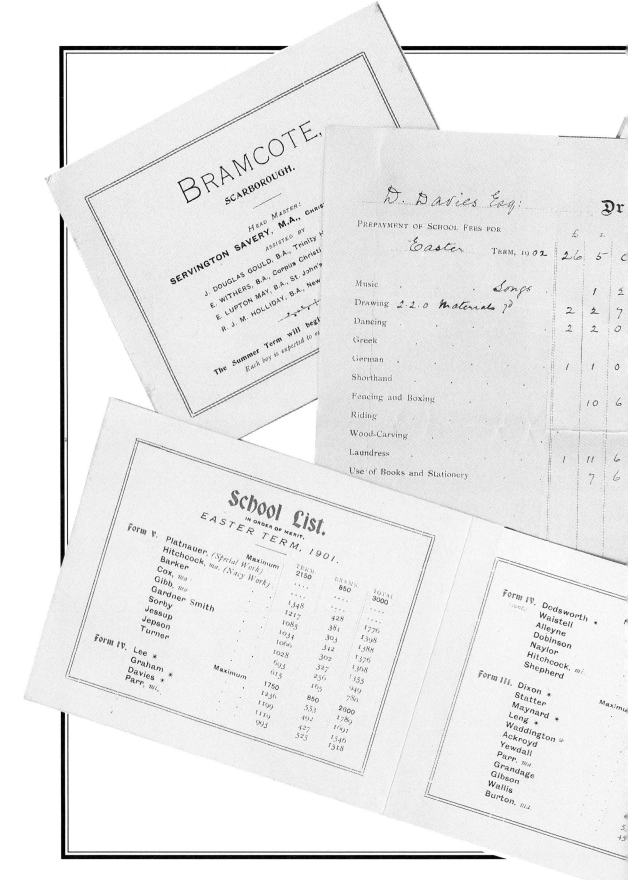

BRAMCOTE,
SCARBOROUGH.

HEAD MASTER:
SERVINGTON SAVERY, M.A., CHRIST

ASSISTED BY
J. DOUGLAS GOULD, B.A., Trinity H
E. WITHERS, B.A., Corpus Christi
E. LUPTON MAY, B.A., St. John's
R. J. M. HOLLIDAY, B.A., New

The Summer Term will begi
Each boy is expected to re

D. Davies Esq.   Dr

PREPAYMENT OF SCHOOL FEES FOR

Easter   TERM, 19 02   26 5 0

	£	s.	
Music . . . Songs		1	
Drawing 2.2.0 Materials 7d	2	2	7
Dancing	2	2	0
Greek . . .			
German . . .	1	1	0
Shorthand .			
Fencing and Boxing		10	6
Riding .			
Wood-Carving .			
Laundress .	1	11	6
Use of Books and Stationery		7	6

School List.
IN ORDER OF MERIT.
EASTER TERM, 1901.

		Maximum TERM. 2150	EXAMS. 850	TOTAL 3000
Form V.	Platnauer, (Special Work)	....	....	
	Hitchcock, ma. (Navy Work)	....	....	
	Barker	....	....	
	Cox, ma.	1348	428	1776
	Gibb, ma.	1217	381	1598
	Gardner Smith	1085	303	1388
	Sorby	1034	342	1376
	Jessup	1066	302	1368
	Jepson	1028	327	1355
	Turner	693	256	949
Form IV.	Lee *	615	165	780
	Graham *	Maximum 1750	850	2600
	Davies *	1236	553	1789
	Parr, mi.	1199	492	1691
		1119	427	1546
		993	525	1518

Form IV.	Dodsworth *
(cont.)	Waistell
	Alleyne
	Dobinson
	Naylor
	Hitchcock, mi.
	Shepherd
Form III.	Dixon *
	Statter
	Maynard *
	Leng *
	Waddington *
	Ackroyd
	Yewdall
	Parr, ma.
	Grandage
	Gibson
	Wallis
	Burton, ma.

Maximum

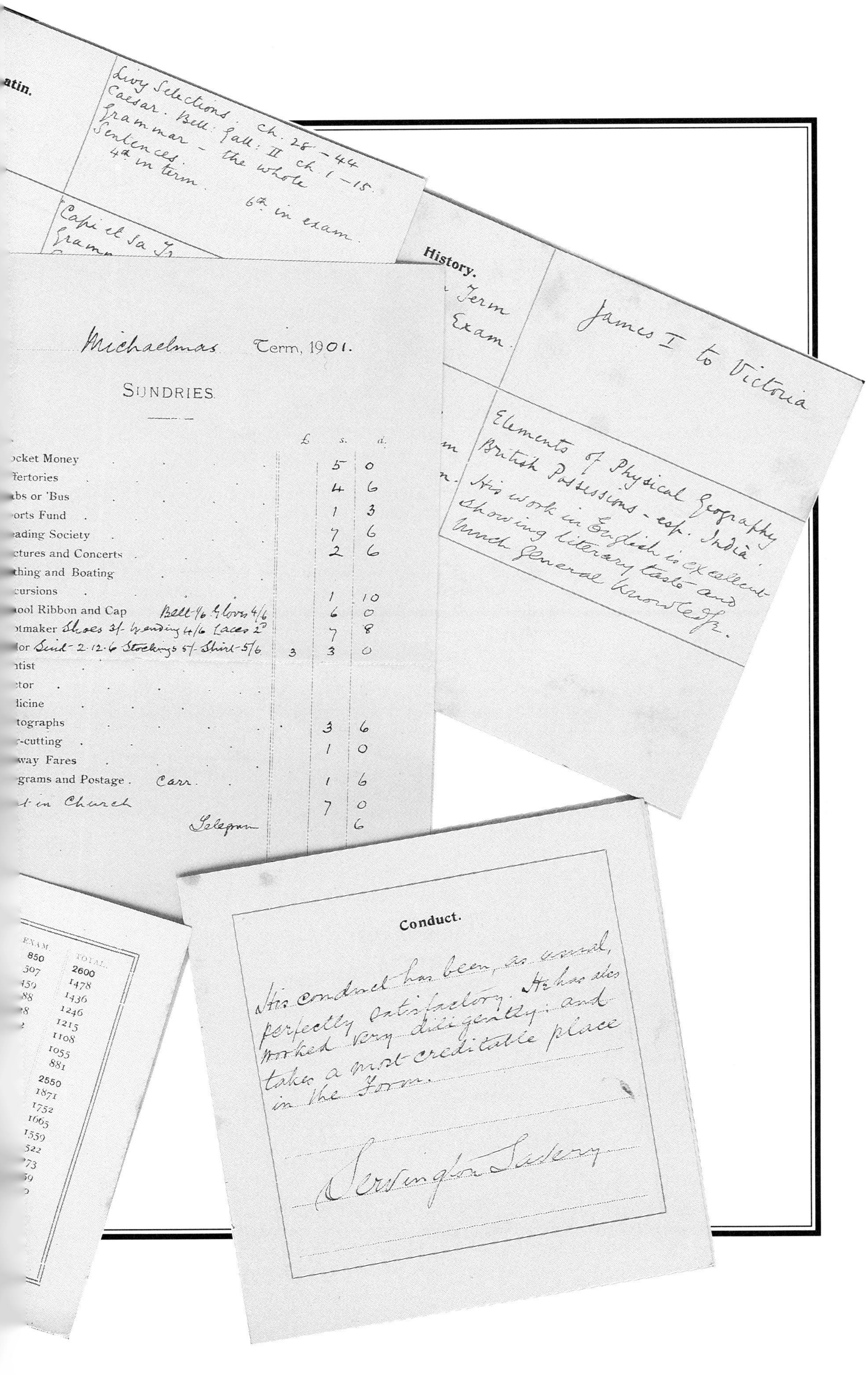

Livy Selections i Ch. 28 - 44.
Caesar. Bell: Gall: II Ch 1 - 15.
Grammar - the whole
Sentences.
4th in term.
6th in exam.

Capic el sa Jr
Gram

History.

Term
Exam

James I to Victoria

Elements of Physical Geography
British Possessions - esp. India.
His work in English is excellent
showing literary taste and
much general knowledge.

Michaelmas Term, 1901.

SUNDRIES.

	£	s.	d.
ocket Money		5	0
ertories		4	6
abs or 'Bus		1	3
orts Fund		7	6
ading Society		2	6
ctures and Concerts			
thing and Boating			
cursions		1	10
ool Ribbon and Cap Bell 4/ Gloves 4/6	1	6	8
otmaker Shoes 3/ Mending 4/6 Laces 2d		7	8
lor Suit 2·12·6 Stockings 5/ Shirt 5/6	3	3	0
ntist			
tor			
dicine			
otographs		3	6
-cutting		1	0
way Fares			
grams and Postage . Carr.		1	6
t in Church		7	0
Telegram			6

EXAM.	TOTAL.
850	2600
507	1478
459	1436
88	1246
8	1215
2	1108
	1055
	881
	2550
	1871
	1752
	1665
	1559
	522
73	
59	

Conduct.

His conduct has been, as usual,
perfectly satisfactory. He has also
worked very diligently, and
takes a most creditable place
in the Form.

Servington Savery

Savery encouraged singing, according to Dodsworth, and there were school concerts, as far as he could remember, every term, with masters and boys singing solos and when a play was often acted. He continued:

The chief concert was on the evening of the Fathers' Match, and the soloists were allowed to join the guests in the dining room for light refreshments. After evening prayers on Sunday those who enjoyed singing stayed on and sang hymns, with Mr Savery at the piano, each boy taking it in turn to sing a verse.

The teaching of English – particularly the appreciation and proper use of our mother-tongue – was in those days a neglected subject. On the other hand classics and mathematics were very well taught indeed. For me classics at Bramcote recall Mr Ling's name. So thoroughly did he ground me in Greek grammar that by the time I left I was not easily defeated. In my time boys were not encouraged to take things easily at Bramcote, and the standard of work was, I should say, above the average. Boys taking chemistry and physics used to attend the laboratory at the Municipal School on the Valley Bridge.

There was little or no real coaching for games and I have no recollection at all of any nets for cricket and, worse still, we played no other schools either at football or cricket. I always heard this was due to the fact that there had been a 'scene' at a school match and Mr Savery decided that he would not risk another. We played no rugger. The Fathers' Match was the main feature of the cricket season, and we used to have some amusing 'Test Trials' between the potential 1st XI and the masters, who only batted five strong, but were allowed to supplement their fielding resources with the next best boys. I remember Mr Savery in one of these games making a tremendous square-leg hit right out of the ground which smashed the window of a house in Holbeck Hill.

It is not easy for me to give a boy's appreciation of Mr Savery as a headmaster, as I have known him so well as a friend in more recent years. I should say quite definitely that he was a firm disciplinarian and that evil-doers had reason to fear him. At the same time, when a boy had his punishment, he was instantly forgiven and the black mark against him expunged. I remember that on one occasion Mr Savery offered several malefactors, including myself, the choice of a beating or an imposition in the form of some arithmetical problems. About 50 per cent including myself, chose the beating; whereupon Mr Savery let us off the beating, but made those who had chosen the sums do the imposition. He always used to impress upon us that 'sneaking' was the one unforgivable sin and tale-bearers used to catch it hot from him. He was always good for a joke.

Before Church each boy was inspected by Miss Savery and teeth and nails carefully examined. Failure to reach the necessary standard of cleanliness was penalised by bad marks, for which a financial forfeit was exacted, the proceeds, I believe, going to Scarborough Hospital. We never went for a walk between Church and dinner, but always in the afternoon, unless it was wet, when Miss Savery read to us. Prayers were at 6.30 p.m., followed by either reading or recitation by Mr Savery.

'Everything was done to create a good "Image",' wrote Rev. P. Gardner-Smith. 'On Sundays we were marched top-hatted and Eton suited to St Martin's, where we filled the south aisle. At other times we always wore brown caps with a gold badge.' The gold badge was Savery's own crest of an eagle. This was changed to 'BS' when Savery left.

12. Above: Bagshawe in Eton Sunday best.
13. Right: Gardner-Smith in the weekday uniform.

From Savery, Slater and Pidcock bought the buildings that have remained at the heart of the school ever since. Originally Savery had purchased a house in Filey Road which he called Bramcote Lodge. He was not satisfied with this, however:

When I found that a new building was necessary, I called in William Robson of Scarborough who had built Bramcote Lodge. He agreed to erect a building for the school according to my plan provided that, if necessary, it could be eventually turned into two houses. He was evidently doubtful as to the future of the school. The basement was opened up to allow for the gym. In May 1898 the new Bramcote was opened with 24 boys, and the original house, being vacated, was taken by Miss Field-Hall who opened her school there under the name of High Cliff. In 1903 Miss Field-Hall moved to new premises and Bramcote Lodge again became part of the school. The buildings were then connected by a corridor over which two small bedrooms and a bathroom and WC were built.

Playing accommodation was found for cricket in a field on the Filey Road and, for football, in a field on which No.2 Weaponness Park is built. With the new premises, a gravel playground and two fives courts were added. In 1900 both fields were taken for building purposes.

On April 4th, 1901 the following notice was sent to the parents: 'Mr Savery desires to announce that he has secured on a long lease the whole of the North of England Lawn Tennis Ground which adjoins his premises. This will be known in future as Bramcote Playing Field and it will be used by the school exclusively for cricket, football, hockey and other sports.'

This notice found its way into the local press; and created some sensation. Correspondence and leading articles were devoted to it. The *Yorkshire Post* spread the outcry of bewilderment and dismay that the town should have lost such an opportunity.

When Savery took over the tennis ground he turned it into five acres of prime playing field – one of the finest to be enjoyed by any such school in the North of England. (The school finally bought the field in the mid 1920s.)

Sir Samuel Savery died in December 1938 and was cremated following a funeral service at Cheltenham Parish Church where Slater represented the school along with three old boys, George Bagshawe, Major Geoffrey Kitson from Leeds and Lionel Kitson from London. At the Memorial Service held later the Vicar of St Mary's Church, Beverley, commented:

'In days gone by Samuel Servington Savery exerted a great Christian influence on many young lives that came under his care at Bramcote and when he retired he did not spend the rest of his life in idleness or futility, but continued to practise what for 20 years he had preached. In an ever-increasing multiplicity of public duties, he maintained that youthfulness of outlook and buoyancy of heart that were always among his most attractive charms.'

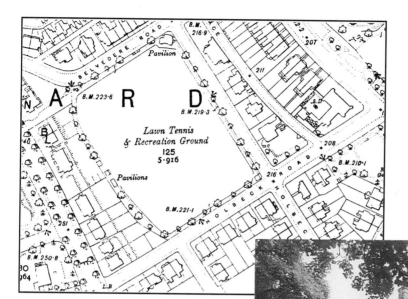

14. *Ordnance Survey map of 1912 showing Netherbank (N); and Bramcote Lodge (BL) by then linked to the new house.*
15. *The 'new house' as it is now.*
16. *The architect's drawings for the new house built by William Robson. (*The Fishing Robsons, *by Peter Robson, p.121, Newby Books, Scarborough.)*

17. *'The Boer war was a good time for us,' said Lumley Dodsworth. 'Mr Savery commemorated any substantial victory over the Boers either by a picnic or a half-holiday.' The picnic was often held by the pub at Hayburn Wyke and they went there by train. On one occasion, he recalled, the engine of the train was decorated all over with Union Jacks for the Relief of Ladysmith.*

18. *'The sports were always serious affairs. Mothers would arrive in their very best clothes and their hats.' (Bagshawe).*

19. The parlour maids serving tea in 1912.

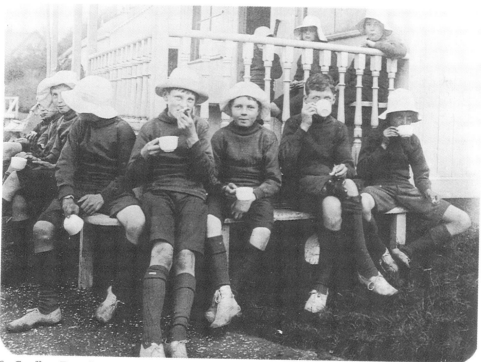

20. Geoffrey Fennell, William Griffiths, George Kitson and Geoffrey Fisher in 1911. After 1909, those boys who were in school teams, could wear their colours on their floppy hats.

21-24. *Many of the traditional features of the Sports Day took shape very early in the history of the school.*

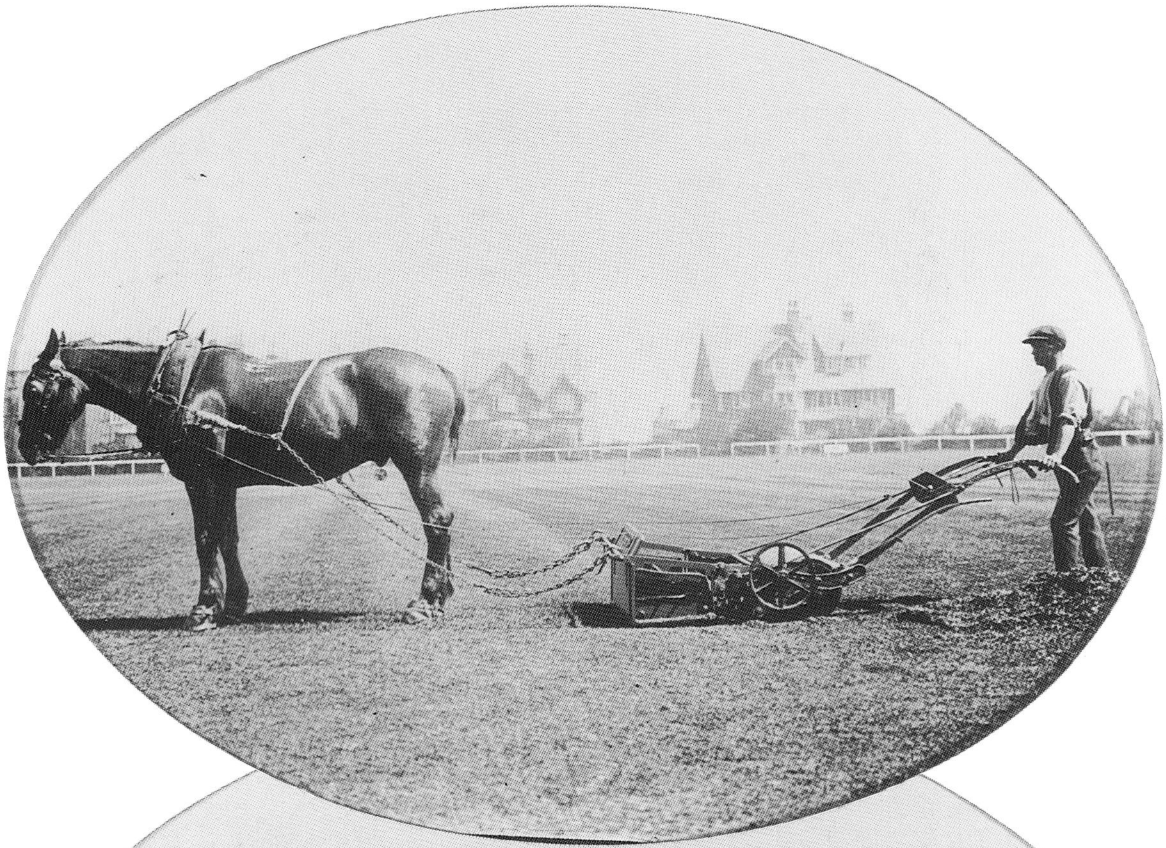

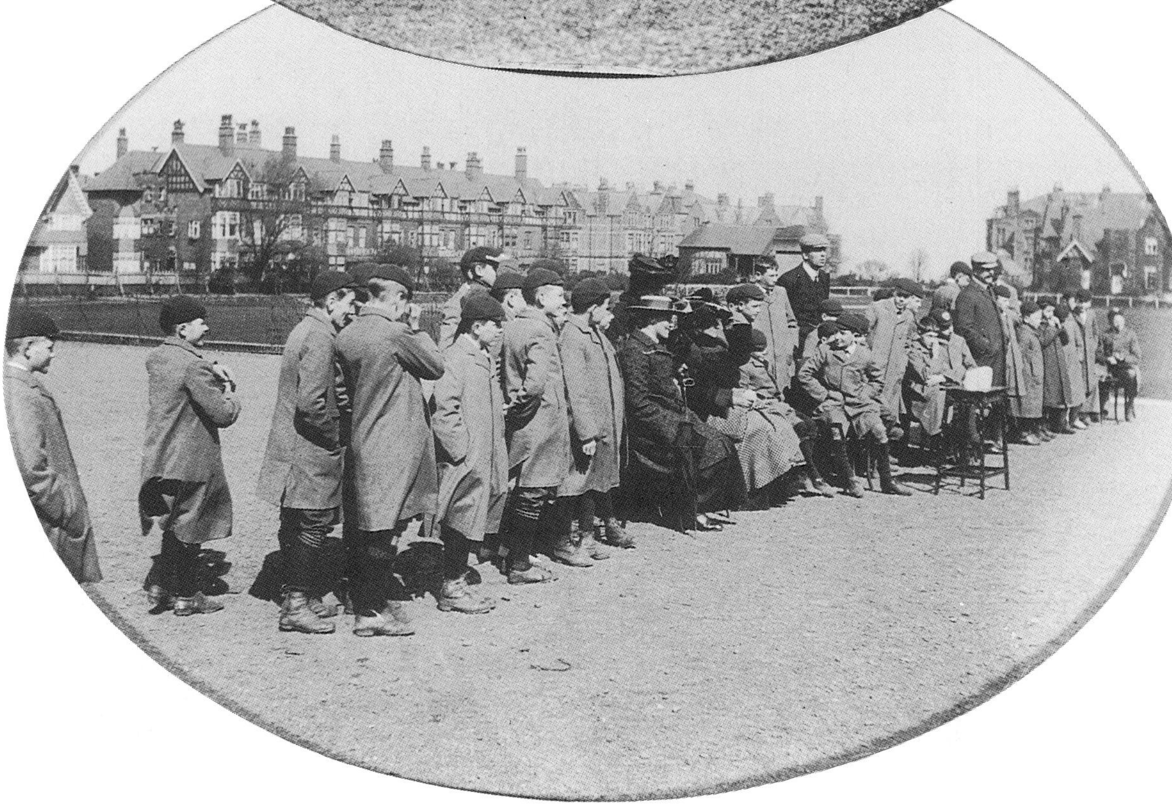

25. Top left: The horse-drawn lawnmower. Bagshawe remembered the horse in 1910 being stabled in what is now the tractor shed.
26. Bottom left: The first photograph, c. 1905, of macs and caps. Macs, caps and round the square (MCRS) is still an institution on wet days, albeit in anoraks now.
27. Below: The school in 1910, Savery in the centre, with Slater seated to his right, and Pidcock to his left. Hemming, is standing on the far right. As a young man he rarely faced the camera.

28. *Savery at the beach with the boys around 1905.*

29. *Slater wrote 'Sunday Afternoon' under this photograph in 1912. The magazine Edward Master is holding is entitled* Railway Travel Monthly.

30. *'I remember going twice by horse-drawn char-a-bancs to Filey for matches,' said Bagshawe. 'Every time we came to a hill we had to push.'*

31. *Football on the field around 1905.*

It wasn't until Pidcock and Slater joined the school that matches with rival prep schools became a regular feature of Bramcote life. Slater wrote of the one against Orleton House on November 3rd, 1909:

'This, our first match, was played on our ground. No wind. No sun. Ground wet and heavy. Pidcock referee. The result was a draw of one goal apiece; from our point of view, the game was exciting throughout, as, for quite two-thirds of the game, we were within shooting distance of their goal: however, owing to the horribly feeble play of our inside forwards in front of goal, we gave away our chances of a win time after time.'

Their first match against Aysgarth was on November 27th, 1909. Both the 1st and 2nd XIs from Bramcote lost. When they went to Aysgarth on December 15th they lost again by two goals to one, as Slater reported:

'We had a very pleasant outing to Aysgarth, in spite of the long journey and getting defeated. The unpleasantness of the former was partially done away with by our having a saloon and no-one could have been very upset about the latter, as it was such a jolly good game and all our side played so well. Burton in goal was magnificent, and Carr at centre half played a fine game. The forwards showed more dash than usual, and even looked like shooting once or twice! Mitchell marked his man well. The backs got through some hard, if somewhat erratic, tackling.' Bramcote lost their first cricket match against Aysgarth too.

It was not till December 1910 that Slater could write: 'It has been a long time coming, but it has come at last – a 1st X1 victory against Aysgarth: and there will never be a better deserved victory. Carr and every member of the side played magnificently and with the exception of the first ten minutes, they played better football in every way than their opponents.'

This rivalry with the Wensleydale school became more intense in 1919 when a friend of Pidcock's from his Winchester and Oxford days, Frank Joy, became headmaster at Aysgarth.

Several of the 1909 football team (Stanley Carr, Archibald Paul, Arthur Broadbent, Eric Bedwell, Christopher Burton, Joseph Mitchell and Henry Bolckow) were also selected for the 1910 1st X1 cricket team along with Derrick Childe and Philip Mackay. Francis Hicking was chosen to play with this team in an away match against Southcliffe on June 11th, 1910 although he is not in the team photograph. Pidcock commented that Southcliffe's ground was small, the outfield a meadow, but the wicket was quite good. The Bramcote bowlers particularly got the better of the Southcliffe batsmen which helped them win by 70 runs. Hicking and Burton hit 30 valuable runs together during the first innings and bowled well, reported Pidcock who also recorded in the Match Book: 'Carr, Mackay, Childe and Hicking all played decent cricket.' These four were to die in the First World War, as was Mitchell.

All those in the 1910 team enlisted. Broadbent was awarded the Military Cross after being wounded twice while serving with the 5th W. Riding Regiment. Burton was a tank commander; Bedwell a wireless telegraphist with the Royal Navy; Paul and Bolckow were Dragoon Guards; and Edward Batty was a lieutenant with a siege battery.

For Bagshawe the First World War in Scarborough began with glass cascading into the dining room just feet away from where he was about to eat breakfast.

32. Preparing for a match around 1912.

33. Cricket First XI, 1910. Back row: Bolckow, Childe, Mitchell. Standing in front of them: Batty, Burton, Bedwell. Sitting: Carr, Paul (Capt), Broadbent. On the ground: Mackay and Wallis.

Through the mist on December 16th, 1914 Pidcock had seen the flash of the canons from two German battlecruisers as they began their bombardment of the East coast. Pidcock wrote in the School Register:

'The house opposite to us, Dunollie, was badly hit and a maid in it blown to pieces. Our postman was killed by the flagstaff at Dunollie garden and our letters were stained with his blood. A fragment of a shell burst back through my sitting room window and made a dent in the wall.' This was preserved for many years to the fascination of decades of boys. The playground was thickly strewn with fragments of shells. 'It was rather frightening to small boys – and to Douglas Slater whom I can picture looking delicate pea-green!' wrote Dr Geoffrey Eddison. Initially the headmasters had ushered the boys into the gym in the basement but this gave little additional protection from the bombardment.

'The headmasters decided that there might very easily be a landing with further ships arriving at any moment,' Bagshawe said, 'So everybody was told to get an overcoat and put their boots on and we were taken onto the golf course at the back of the Filey Road and there we stayed for a couple of hours.' Before they left, however, according to Dr Eddison, they were told to grab some food as they had never eaten breakfast. 'I distinctly remember getting a banana from somewhere or somebody which I ate while we were made to walk, in company with the girls from the school next door, to the golf course.'

As the battlecruisers had moved on up the coast the boys were taken back to the school. Bagshawe continued: 'We got back to the school about 12 o'clock and the headmasters decided that in case there was a landing at a later date the boys should be sent home. Between 12 o'clock and 5 o'clock a bag was packed – an overnight bag – and the boys' parents were telephoned where possible that the boy would be coming home on a train that night. The whole school left Scarborough at 5 o'clock at night and they had to make the best way they could to their homes. On our own – in the dark. I had with me one of the youngest boys in the school called Rhodes – he lived in Huddersfield and so when we got to Leeds where I was going I had to take him to another station and put him on a train for Huddersfield which I did. I would be 12 then. The next day Mr Slater received a telephone message from a very fussy parent – to say that her boy had arrived without a shirt and would they please send it on at once.'

Following this attack the school was moved to Bradfield, Berkshire for about a year. The battlecruisers had also bombarded Hartlepool and Whitby that day; 124 people were killed and over 500 injured, providing a major propaganda victory to the Germans. Within two days the Army appealed to young men: 'Avenge Scarborough – Up and At 'Em Now'[1].

The school's Roll of Honour listed 171 Old Bramcotians who fought in the First World War, all but 12 of whom had left the school by the summer of 1911 (by which time 239 boys had been enrolled at Bramcote). Nine masters also enlisted, three of whom were killed. Pidcock enlisted in 1917 and became a 2nd Lt. with the 5th Battalion of the King's Royal Rifles. He was wounded on September 29th, 1918. While he was away Slater was assisted by G.A. Coller, an old friend. Pidcock wrote later: 'The difficulties of staff during the war may be seen from the Register and we were very lucky to have three first class men

[1] Dissertation by R.L. Feather, January 1989

(Hemming, Stewart and Roach) who were either too old or unfit to be soldiers.' He returned to the school in January 1919. The School Register at that time listed eight staff besides Slater and Coller, four of whom were women. The staff numbers did not increase much throughout the early twenties. Among those who returned from the war were Jack Alleyne (Lt. Sir John Alleyne Bt.) and Charles Geoffrey Vickers VC.

2nd Lt. Vickers – then a temporary Captain – was awarded the Victoria Cross for holding a trench in the Hohenzollern redoubt against heavy odds the day after his 21st birthday. The citation read: 'When nearly all his men had been killed or wounded, and with only two men available to hand him bombs, Captain Vickers held a barrier for some hours against heavy German bomb attacks from front and flank. By ordering a second barrier to be built for the safety of the trench, he knowingly cut off his own retreat. He was severely wounded but he saved a critical situation.' There was probably only one other survivor of that incident – Private John Bullivant DCM – who wrote later:

'The redoubt was practically won by Captain Vickers. You wouldn't think a man could have done what he did. The Germans were doing their best to kill him but he stuck to the work until a barricade had been made, and would not leave the place. He was very daring and I thought every minute he would be blown to pieces, but even when he had been wounded he would not come away till the barricade was properly established. The enemy were only about twenty yards away and were continually throwing bombs, but Captain Vickers never wavered and was still fighting when I had to leave as I had been hit.'

Vickers' was the first VC to be awarded to the 7th (Robin Hood) Sherwood Foresters, Nottingham's Territorial Regiment and he was given a hero's welcome when he returned to the city in February 1916. He was also awarded the Croix de Guerre. In the 1939-45 war, Col Vickers served in staff appointments on the National Emergency Committee and in the field of Economic Intelligence. A qualified solicitor, he worked on the Board of London Transport and the National Coal Board, and was honoured with a Knighthood. He died in March 1982.

Jack Alleyne only just survived the war and his rescue from a ship off Ostend in May 1918 was graphically portrayed on the front cover of a newspaper called *The Sphere*. He had been involved in the scuttling of two ships in order to block Ostend harbour. He wrote to his brother when recuperating in hospital in France:

'We steamed up and down about a mile or so either way three or four times, until suddenly we sighted the pier heads close to S.W. and I think they must have seen us about the same time, as the fire began to concentrate on us then, and we started getting hit. We made for the entrance and just as we were coming up to the piers, they opened a pretty hot fire on us with machine guns. The Captain and I were on the bridge, so as we came up to the piers, the Captain said we would go down to the conning tower; so we started down, but I got hit by a machine gun bullet just as I got down the first ladder. It hardly hurt at all [a button deflected the bullet which went through his waist] but made me feel horribly sick and shaky at the knees almost at once.' Another ML managed to reach their stricken ship and rescue them, even though one of their officers and several men had been killed. In the Second World War he captained three Armed Merchant Cruisers.

Head Masters:

R. D. Slater, M.A.,
Wellington, and Univ. Coll., Oxford.

R. G. Pidcock, M.A.,
Winchester, and New Coll., Oxford;

*For seven years Assistant-Masters at "Summer Fields,"
near Oxford.*

BOYS are received between the ages of seven and fourteen, in order to train them for the Public Schools, and for the Royal Navy. For this purpose a large and well-appointed house has been built in the best part of Scarborough. It is situated on the South Cliff, at the foot of Oliver's Mount. The rooms are light and lofty, there is ample lavatory and bathroom accommodation, and the building is fitted with an indoor Gymnasium and all modern conveniences. There is a separate Sanatorium adjoining and looking on to the playing field. No day-boys are received.

34. 1919 prospectus.

The Boys attend Church on Sunday mornings, and a Short Service is held in the School on Sunday evenings.

SCHOOL HOURS

Prayers	-	8-45 a.m.
First School	-	9 a.m. until 11
Second ,,	-	11-30 ,, 1-0
Third ,,	-	2-30 p.m. ,, 4-0
Prayers	-	6-15
Preparation	-	6-30 ,, 7-30

In Winter the Third School begins at 4 o'clock. The lower forms do no preparation.

The Headmasters are assisted by a staff of four resident University Graduates and a Governess.

The work is arranged with a view to preparing boys to take a creditable place in any Public School or Osborne. The subjects of instruction are Scripture, the usual English subjects, Latin, Greek, French, Arithmetic, Algebra, Geometry. Class singing is also taught.

Great importance is attached to clear handwriting, and to neatness in all written work; boys are encouraged from the beginning, to learn, and maintain, good habits of order and neatness.

Open Scholarships have been won at many of the Public Schools; and several boys have gained Naval Cadetships at Osborne. A list of recent successes is enclosed.

TERMS   -   -   Forty-five Guineas per Term.

....

EXTRAS

Piano - - - -	Two guineas per Term.
Riding - - - -	Three ,, ,,
Drawing - - - -	Two ,, ,,
Dancing - - -	Two ,, ,,
Carpentering - - -	Two ,, ,,
Laundress - - -	One and a half ,,
Use of School Books, Papers, Stationery, and Library - - }	One Guinea ,,

....

The Fees are payable in advance, at the beginning of each Term, in September, January, and May.

No reduction is made for absence owing to illness or other causes.

A Term's notice, or a Term's fees, will be required before the removal of a pupil.

SPORTS AND PHYSICAL TRAINING

The Headmasters and the Staff take an active part in all the games. The playing field, which is immediately attached to the premises, comprises more than five acres of perfectly level turf; in addition, there is a good-sized dry playground, with Fives Courts, and outside Gymnasium. Association and Rugby Football are both played in the Winter terms, and in Summer, besides Cricket, a certain amount of Lawn Tennis. There are good facilities in Scarborough for learning Riding and Swimming, and every boy is taught to swim. Weekly instruction is given in Boxing and Physical Drill.

DOMESTIC MANAGEMENT

The domestic arrangements are under the supervision of a Lady Housekeeper. An experienced Matron looks after the boys' health. Great care is paid to every detail of health especially in the case of delicate boys.

Breakfast is at - -	8	o'clock.
Lunch ,, -	11	,,
Dinner ,, -	1-15	,,
Tea ,, -	5-30	,,
Supper ,, -	7-30	,,

CHAPTER 2

The Consolidation of Excellence
1920–1939

Pidcock was the man who made Bramcote, said Bevan Gamble who taught at the school for 126 terms from 1930 until 1977. 'He was a very great man. He took a terrific interest in everything. He had very high standards and was a deeply religious man. It was such a pleasant atmosphere. You were mixing with very nice people. I don't remember arguments or quarrels among the staff – certainly not in the pre-war years. You got to know each other and helped each other out if necessary. There was no jealousy or backbiting.'

During the 1920s and 1930s there were between 65 and 75 boys a year at the school and a steady flow of scholarships into leading Public Schools. The curriculum covered Latin (composition and verses), Greek, French, mathematics, English (including literature), geography, Scripture and history. Music and drawing were listed as minor options.

The objective was academic excellence, a good sports record and fine manners but, as Bevan Gamble commented: 'In Pidder's day the only thing that counted was a Winchester scholarship.' It was 1929 before Pidcock saw one of his boys gain a first on the Winchester Election Roll – John Humphrey who went on to become Professor (later Emeritus) of Immunology at London University (1976-81). Val Wrigley (1924-29), who got a second at Uppingham the same year, wrote:

'R.G. Pidcock, in my view, was one of the great prep school headmasters. He was one of those dedicated men who gave his whole life to the job. It was the quality of teaching and the pressure to learn – and to learn thoroughly – which left the most abiding impression. The staff was academically well qualified – mostly Public School and Oxbridge – and of course was much aided by the small classes which varied in size from seven to 13 or so. Pidcock was a marvellous and thorough teacher of classics, history and divinity.' Val Wrigley, who became a headmaster himself, was amazed at how much Pidcock did, especially after Slater left in 1925 and until Oswald Cooper joined him in the partnership in 1930.

'Pidcock paid the staff, taught, got us up in the morning to our compulsory cold baths, taught us cricket in the nets and during the fielding practice at break (he was a fine cricketer) and took us to church,' Val Wrigley explained. And on Sundays Pidcock kept up the correspondence with parents.

For the boys, life was completely full observed Canon Gervase Markham. 'It was like being part of an ant hill. One went on doing the things that were set down for one. There were certain things we had to do which were valuable. One was the custom in the top class of a lot of quotations from the Bible being written up at the beginning of the week. You had to use your own ingenuity to find where they came from, who did it. We got to know our Bibles very well. I still regard these as stock phrases you should know from the Bible.' In September 1923 he wrote home that Pidcock had just invented this new idea. Some of the 20 verses they had worked on that week were: 'My name is Legion'; 'What I have now done? Is there not a cause'; and 'Blessed are they that have not seen and yet have believed'. Pidcock's system underwent a change, however, in 1930 as Val Wrigley was to witness:

'Oswald Cooper was an historian and the week's "Contexts" on the blackboard from then on used to alternate between Pidcock's biblical quotations one week with Cooper's historical ones the next. We were examined on them on Saturdays and I can still remember most of them.' Those attending the school in the 1940s can recall this system although they said they were allowed to use a concordance for the biblical quotations.

By the time he became headmaster Oswald Cooper had already been at Bramcote for ten years. He, like Pidcock, was a Wykehamist. A graduate of Oriel College, Oxford, he served with the Lancashire Fusiliers in the First World War rising to the rank of Captain. In 1918 he married Beatrice King and in 1919 spent a year teaching at Uppingham.

35. *'Pidcock had class,' commented John Cundall. 'He used to come round the dormitories after dinner dressed in his plum jacket smoking Balkan Sobranie. There was this waft of cigarette smoke as he passed. That's Pidcock the Patriarch – with the fifth form in 1936. That's my brother, Henry Cundall, on the far left, and (I think) Jim Hornby beside him. Roderick Campbell is on the far right.' The others were Robert Hone, Alistair Denny and Ian Graham.*

In 1919 the Canon Markham Snr was considering sending his son Gervase to Bramcote. He wrote therefore to a friend, Canon Cecil Cooper in Scarborough, who had two sons (Paul and Martin) at the school. Canon Cooper replied:

Dear Canon Markham,

I am afraid that you write to a person who is rather prejudiced in the matter of Bramcote, as both my boys are there and the two Headmasters are personal friends of ours. Mr Pidcock was a Winchester man when my father in law was Dean of Winchester and I was Rector there. Mr Slater is an old Wellingtonian. I consider Bramcote an excellent school – with a sound manly tone, and distinctly out of true Religion and loyal Churchmanship. The masters I mention are regular communicants weekly and men of delightfully clean and manly influence.

The one thing about the school is that it is not in any way luxurious. The food is very good my boys say but cold baths and regular public school hardness is the spirit of the school. There is an excellent Nurse and Matron. Scholarship is attended to and their record at Winchester is good – and every care is taken to make them good athletes too. The boys go to St Martin's Church to Matins (not Choral Eucharist) and the vicar teaches there once a week. His boy is also at Bramcote.

Winchester College is very glad to get Bramcote boys . . . Personally I think it is one of the best Preparatory Schools in the Country and I know a good many in the South. If you want your son to enter you will have to decide soon as they are booked up till 1921!

Writing letters to parents each term took the place then of the full term report. In November 1920 Mrs Markham received this communication from Pidcock:

Dear Mrs Markham,

I am v. sorry Canon Markham cannot come. I will certainly have a word with you about Gervase at half term. I should say the general result is quite satisfactory. I will get further opinions from those who take him before you come. He comes every Sunday morning to my room with a list of his various places which I keep on a card. By this means I keep myself pretty well informed of what he is at. Of course one does not want to overwork him as he is not yet 10, but one doesn't want to develop slack habits and find himself unsound in elementary things when he gets higher in the school. He seems very well. I have great hopes he will become not only a scholar but also a good footer [football] player.

April 3, 1923

Dear Canon Markham,

A line about Gervase. Please answer at your leisure but I should rather like to know at the beginning of next term what your plans are for his future. Is the idea of Winchester in any case with or without a scholarship or a scholarship somewhere if it can be got? I know he doesn't leave till July '24, but I find it more satisfactory to have an idea as to the plan of campaign. I may have over-estimated his ability but I have always expected him to be better than he is and my view is shared by all the staff except perhaps Slater. All the rest of us think he could do rather better and whether we are right or wrong, it is an opinion which has been arrived at unwillingly, as G. is a very popular gentleman with the whole staff and they certainly don't set out to 'crab' him. I beat him one day about a month ago as I was quite clear he was definitely idle & I had spoken to him about it before. I like the boy most awfully and I want him to do well. Personally I hope you decide to send him to Winchester anyhow as he should be a very good member of society there but I don't feel at all confident that he can get a Winchester scholarship. If you don't want to come to a decision just yet, I should like to know what is passing in your mind.

Yours sincerely,
Richard Pidcock.

Gervase Markham's Easter Term report that year recorded comments like: Eng.Lit – only fair at present; History – apparently a weak subject; Latin comp and verses – poor at present; Geography – he should be making more headway. Obviously dismayed, his parents wrote again to Canon Cooper who replied:

My dear Markham,

Honestly I don't attach much importance to Bramcote reports. I love Slater and Pidcock dearly. They are true sane good men – but their standard is very high indeed and they err on the side of severity of standard. I know they loved my two boys but constantly we had reports which depressed me! Until I knew them exacting pedagogues.
I happen to know that they love your little chap and think a lot of him. Don't worry. Tell Gervase to do his level best – that's all. Let him have a shot for Winchester as my Martin had his shot last June and God bless the result. Slater and Pidcock are two of the best laymen in the world – but they aren't infallible.

From 1910 until 1925 the joint headmaster system meant that Slater and Pidcock could share out the workload of caring for the boys and writing to their parents. 'I was Slater's boy. Pidcock didn't have anything to do with me,' George Bagshawe said. 'Everybody liked Pidcock but Slater was rather unreasonable.'

Even so, it was Slater who aroused his interest in acting. Bagshawe played the principal role in one school play produced by Slater and he emphasised: 'You were taught to act properly.' In 1927, 12 years after he left Bramcote, Bagshawe began acting, as an amateur, with the Leeds Rep and the Leeds Civic Playhouse. At the latter he met an American actress and they were married within six weeks. 'Friends said it would never last but we were happily married for 45 years,' he chuckled.

It was Slater who schooled Gervase Markham as to how he should behave in church. 'On my first Sunday I had to go to Mr Slater and he enquired whether I had ever been to church before. He said: "Well now, there are certain things we do. You must remember that when we say the Creed you stand up to attention, put your heels together and hands down." And I was rehearsed in doing that. Ever since for the rest of my life I have felt wrong if I have not had my heels together when I have said the Apostles' Creed.' Like George Bagshawe, Canon G. Markham also recalled Slater being very good at teaching them elocution.

'I remember now the importance attached to speaking each word separately and being taught how to pronounce the final consonant of a word. So few are taught that nowadays and that is why so many public speakers are inaudible. But I learnt it early and I have valued it ever since. He was devoted to the boys. He knew exactly what had happened to all the boys in the school.' He recalled being chastised by Slater for not learning his Latin, without being beaten. But others remembered Slater very differently, even Val Wrigley:

'Slater was much feared for his sarcasm, his readiness to cane on the hand for the smallest mistake and for his marking system. In the third form two marks were the maximum for a Latin sentence, but we lost one mark straightaway if there was no full stop and one came off for every other mistake, so some boys regularly gave in minus marks. We received no encouragement from him, but certainly never made the same mistake twice. I learned one valuable lesson, however, when I myself came to teach, never to use sarcasm as a way of handling children.'

Slater left schooling altogether in 1925, a year after his marriage. 'He married the widowed mother of my great friend at the school, A.M. Rendel,' said Canon G. Markham. 'She was a nice motherly type.'

When Slater married he bought another house next door to the school buildings – Netherbank. This also had been built by William Robson and had the distinctive dentilled cornice. After he retired he gave the house to the school. Today three of the rooms on the ground floor are used as classrooms. Above these are dormitories – and in the 'servants' quarters' live three bachelor masters. But back in the late 1920s the story was very different . . .

'I joined Bramcote as a dormitory maid in 1924,' Mrs F. Procter told us in 1993. 'I was 16 – and Mr Hemming was old to me. He was very nice. There were eleven of us women working there then. We were all from Durham. They didn't have Scarborough girls because they didn't stay if they didn't like it. My sister

said I would not stay long when I came. And I am still here.' She married a
Scarborough man in 1928 and now has three children, eight grandchildren and
three great-grandchildren in the area.

'I spent a year working in the main school and then went to work at
Netherbank. I worked with Miss Elsie Berridge. Miss Elsie stayed with me. I was
right at the top with a window overlooking the sea – away from everybody. There
used to be five masters in the whole of Netherbank. They had the dining room
and lounge on the ground floor and the other room was a workroom where the
boys did woodwork. There were the masters' bedrooms upstairs. The masters
came over to the main school for breakfast and lunch and had the evening meal
there. I had to come to the main school in the holidays and stay there and clean
because Netherbank closed down.

'It was hard work compared with what it is now. You had to get all the school
room fires lit – and if you didn't do them in time you missed your breakfast. And
I did several times. But I enjoyed the work.' At Netherbank each week she had to
polish the main staircase and dust it once a day. All the carpets had to be cleaned,
using a brush for there were no vacuum cleaners then. In those years the school
was slowly being converted from gas to electric lighting. Mrs Thomas was in
charge of the housekeeping and Mrs Procter commented:

'She was all right at times but she could be terrible if you didn't do just as she
wanted. We had half a day off a week and every other Sunday. We had to be in at
half past nine or we had Mrs Thomas after us. We had no night life at all. We just
used to go to look around town and we went to church on Sunday morning – to
Christchurch which is not there now.'

36. Netherbank about 1928.

37. *Mrs Thomas watches as the boys clear the field of plaintains.*

38. *Frank Hamerton helps the boys to roll the grass.*

39. On the sledge during the winter of 1929: John Hornsby, John Grier, Henry Cairns-Terry, Martin Phelps, John Douglas-Withers, Michael Edwards and John Dumoulin.

40. John Humphrey, Urling-Smith, Alfred Humphrey, Charles Wrigley and Claude Wright clearing the snow during the same winter.

In 1993 Canon G. Markham recalled: 'We all knew that one day during the summer there would be a picnic to Cayton Bay but nobody knew when it would be coming and there was always an exciting moment when one sunny morning sitting at our desks suddenly the word would come "Cayton Bay" and everything went up in an explosion of delight. All the books were put away, we got our things for the seaside and before very long a motorcoach would appear outside and we all got in and drove along the road. We tumbled out into a sandy gorge leading down to the huge, unspoilt sweep of sand that was Cayton Bay. The first thing was for Slater or Pidcock to produce an enormous jar of sweets and these were handed out a handful for every boy and these were put in your shorts' pockets and were consumed at intervals as these got hairier and hairier from the inside of your pocket in the course of the day. Spades of some sort I suppose were issued and everybody set about digging the biggest sandcastle or the longest trench... I don't remember much swimming but there was much paddling and games of every sort on the beach.'

In 1923 he had written home, with spelling mistakes uncorrected:

Dear Mummy,

On Tuesday we went for a picnic to Cayton Bay, every one in the school went except one of the masters, because we had been singing very well lately. As soon as we got there, just after dinner, we came in charabangs, we bathed. So did Mr Slater and Mr Pidcock. It was fun, and then we got dressed and went to the edge of the sea, and built a huge castle. Then Mr Pidcock came on, he had been playing cricket on the sands and so it got bigger still, till it was about as tall as me. Then it was tea-time. We had sandwiches, buns, a few jam tarts and then, at the end strawberries. There were 2 huge soap boxes full of sandwiches etc. and each boy had about 20 strawberries. While we were having tea, some other children came and trod all over our castle, so Mr Pidcock told me to go and tell them to go away. When we got their, we saw that there mother was there, so I asked her if they could go away. When we had finished, we went back to the castle again, and continued trying to make a moat from the sea to it, because we had not built it near enough to the sea, and it was an awful pity, for just when we were going we saw the tide just reaching it. While I was putting stones on it to make it hard, I had put one stone on, and it had been partly covered by the sand so that, when I was slamming another stone down, I never saw this other one, so I got my 4th finger on my left hand between the 2 stones and I have had it in a bandage. It is just getting better now. Please can you send me some more sweets because I have run out.

Goodbye,
Love from Gervase

41. 'Pidcock was more athletic than Slater and enjoyed joining in the games much more,' Canon G. Markham said. 'Slater was more aloof.' Val Wrigley remembered Pidcock as a very good cricket coach, who bowled off-breaks with a very round-arm action as a result of the war injury in his shoulder.

42. Below: Mrs Thomas, James Stormonth Darling, Pidcock, Anthony Wilkinson, David Hanson, Alfred Mather and Miss Phyllis Elam in 1930.

43. Frank Hamerton was nicknamed 'Shem' at that time because, like the eldest son of Noah, he was the red one. 'He had a brick red complexion and when he wore shorts his legs were marble white. And, of course, as boys we used to speculate where he changed colour,' commented one Old Boy.

44. *Bottom left: 'It was just good fun to be on your knees catching shrimps with the children,' said Bevan Gamble. 'It was a great thrill to get one (a shrimp) – and digging and building sandcastles. There was always something to do – and of course you had to keep an eye on your charges. Miss Elam used to help, and then Miss Bolton and the music mistress, Miss Brightwell. And the Berridges - there was Flo, the cook; Dot who helped with odd things and in the kitchen and Miss Elsie, the housekeeper at Netherbank.' (Miss Elam, who taught English and geography to the younger forms for 13 years left in 1931 and married Dr R. Edmondson.)*

45. *Right: Mrs Thomas providing tea and food. Charles Wrigley said this was the one time he enjoyed the food at Bramcote.*

46. *Teatime on the beach.*

47. Thelwell at the 1933 Cayton Bay picnic.

48. Thelwell (far left) with William Slack, Thelwell's father, Timothy Slack, Graham Mackrill, Mr Mackrill, Thelwell's sister, Cecil Slack, and Ian Mackrill.

Charles Wrigley was not so enamoured with Bramcote as his twin brother, Val. 'I'm afraid that my memories of my five years at Bramcote are far from happy,' he wrote. 'The worst feature of life at Bramcote in those days was the food – small both in quantity and quality. Then came the discipline. Breaches of discipline were rewarded by "six of the best" delivered in Pidcock's study, which left raw, swollen marks on the unfortunate's behind.'

Henry Gillam was even more cryptic: 'I can recall Pidcock. An admirable man. He beat me. Reluctantly on his part because he tried at first to reason with me, but I insisted on a beating. A beating was the equivalent of a duelling scar and the stripes could be proudly displayed at cold bath time the next morning.'

Peter Thelwell (1931-35) was more appreciative: 'I certainly had a great five years at Bramcote and have always been grateful to the grand team who guided me through the most formative years of my life so cheerfully and so well.' But he added, 'On arrival at school I soon found that life was pretty spartan.' He enjoyed playing Fives which was like squash except that they used a small wooden bat as a racquet. 'I have good cause to remember this particular piece of equipment,' he said. 'After some especially heinous crime had been committed by three of us, Dick Hornby, Alastair Denny and I were sentenced to receive three of the best from Pidcock with a Fives bat. The first was bearable, as was the second but, when the third was delivered on the same cheek as the first, it was hard to conceal one's feelings.

'Cold baths and fresh air were considered vital, and I recall that, from a dormitory overlooking one of the bathrooms, we could actually watch Pidcock taking his cold bath every morning. I often wonder if he took his bath with that purpose in mind.'

Peter Terry (1927-32) recounted at least one attempt to alter Pidcock's views: 'There was an article in the *Daily Mirror* of all papers which somebody saw on the matron's table or desk and it said that cold baths were only for people of herculean stature otherwise it didn't do you any good. So this was cut out of the matron's paper and sent to the headmaster – with no effect whatever, I may say.'

There was little in the way of interesting activities outside school hours in those days. When the boys did have some spare time many of them, according to Peter Thelwell, made model boats. The size of the boats was limited by the fact that they had little space in which to store them – either in their lockers or in their desks. Thelwell wrote:

'Outings were few and far between so a visit to the promenade one summer evening to watch the liner *Aquitania* come right into the bay on her way to the breaker's yard is a vivid memory. Occasionally, after playing cricket against Aysgarth at Escrick Park we visited York Minster and the Railway Museum in that City.' In the 1930s Aysgarth-bound teams had travelled by train, recalled Bevan Gamble. They booked their own coach which had to be shunted to another train at York. For some years the station master at York had a son at Bramcote and he always received them with great honour, dressed in his top hat and tails. On the way back they often had a meal at York station and did not reach Scarborough until 9 p.m.

Even though they could not sleep away from school during term time, parents could take them out occasionally. Thelwell's sister was then attending Queen Margaret's School in Scarborough and two families linked up during leave-outs to take some of the children to the beach.

Thelwell tried to model his bowling on that of Peter Terry, which was not so surprising as Terry was one of a very successful cricket team – so successful, in fact, that a special card was printed to commemorate the season of Summer 1932. This team won ten and drew one out of the eleven matches they played (including beating the Fathers by 83 runs). Oswald Cooper wrote to Roderick Cairns-Terry's parents:

'We have never before had two bowlers like him and Terry who have so completely carried the side on their shoulders and the great success we have had this year is largely due to them. Until the last two matches Rod was never taken off in a match and as he takes a longish run and puts all himself into his bowling, it was only to be expected that he was a bit jaded at the end of the term. I am sure if anyone has earned a holiday Rod has. He is a refreshing if not a very sound bat. But he does realise that the ball is there to be hit and does not consider it to be the right tactics to let the bowler attack him. I feel sure he will in later life face the world in the same spirit.' Cooper then went on to discuss Roderick's younger brother, John, stating:

'He has been very keen on his cricket, has made himself a good fielder and shows promise as a bat. At present he would neither play nor work himself to a standstill as Rod would. It is not in his nature, but he is a tenacious little beggar, and I would bet on his achieving anything that he sets out to do. He is becoming a great deal more lively and has been very naughty this term ragging in his bedroom which secretly has pleased me a great deal, though he has often been reproved both verbally and actively for it. I do think at the moment he has rather too placid an outlook on life, and he wants to acquire the power to drive himself more, even though the spirit and body may be weary.'

Such letters showed that Pidcock had renewed the system whereby the joint headmasters divided up the school between them. Now there were 'Cooper's boys' and 'Pidcock's boys'.

Roderick Cairns-Terry was upset with himself when he fell over one day and hurt his leg. He had to be pushed around in a bathchair for some weeks – Henry Yellowlees particularly enjoyed that job. Peter Terry pointed out that four boys from that era at Bramcote went on to be knighted – James Cleminson, James Stormonth Darling, Christopher Foxley-Norris and Henry Yellowlees. Terry added that Harold Lawrie became his brother-in-law and Charles Lawrie a very successful amateur golf player who captained the British Walker Cup team. By 1935 at Bramcote Charles Lawrie, as a senior, won the both the Fives and the Tennis tournaments and had gained his 1st XI cricket colours. One of Terry's abiding memories of playing in the 1st XI was the sausage and mash they had for tea with the opposition team. His cricket team-mate, Marcus Dick, son of a Scarborough doctor, was top of the school by Michaelmas Term 1931 when he was only 11 years old. He remained there until the Summer Term of 1933 when he was first on the Winchester Election Roll.

49. Top right: The 1932 cricket team. Standing: Michael Edwards, John Dumoulin, John Rogerson, John Pallot. Seated: Harold Lawrie, Peter Terry, Alec Taylor, Ralph Turton and Roderick Cairns-Terry. Sitting on ground: Marcus Dick and John Douglas-Withers.
50. Bottom right: Pushing the bathchair in 1933 – Henry Yellowlees, Martin Phelps and Peter Batterbury with James Clerk-Rattray alongside Roderick Cairns-Terry.

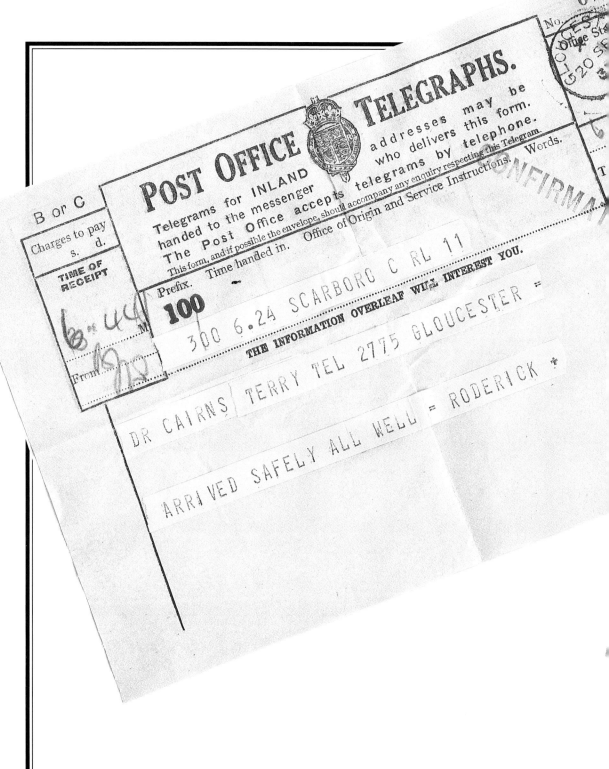

POST OFFICE TELEGRAPHS.

Telegrams for INLAND addresses may be handed to the messenger who delivers this form. The Post Office accepts telegrams by telephone. This form, and if possible the envelope, should accompany any enquiry respecting this Telegram.

B or C

Charges to pay
s. d.

TIME OF RECEIPT

From

Prefix. Time handed in. Office of Origin and Service Instructions. Words.

100 300 6.24 SCARBORO C RL 11

THE INFORMATION OVERLEAF WILL INTEREST YOU.

DR CAIRNS/TERRY TEL 2775 GLOUCESTER =

ARRIVED SAFELY ALL WELL = RODERICK +

51. *In 1928 Roderick Cairns-Terry's parents decided that the local school was so inadequate that they ought to send both Roderick and his older brother, Michael, to Bramcote School, which they had heard about through a relative. It was a long journey from Gloucester with no adult to accompany them. Once they had arrived safely, with their trunks, they sent a telegram to their parents.*

PLEASE FILL IN THIS INVENTORY AND RETURN IN THE BOY'S TRUNK.

SUMMER TERM.

*1 Light Brown Covert Coat
1 Light Brown Raincoat   (If a belt worn, firmly attach)
3 Pyjamas
4 Flannel Shirts   (Without collars, plain or striped)
3 Vests and Pants
6 Pairs of Grey Stockings   (Plain tops)
12 Soft White Collars   ("Polo" or similar kind)
12 Pocket Handkerchiefs
3 Black Silk Eton Ties
2 Pairs of Braces
2 White Sweaters
*1 Grey Woollen "Pull-over,"   to be worn only with
    Flannel Suits
1 Pair of Black Boots or Shoes for best
1 Pair of Brown Boots or Shoes
2 Pairs of Brown Boots or Shoes for rough wear
1 Pair of House Shoes   ("Cambridge")
1 Pair of Black Patent for dancing
    (These may be used as second house shoes)
1 Pair of Bedroom Slippers
1 Pair of White Gym. Shoes
1 Dressing Gown
2 Caps
1 Belt
1 Bible and Prayer Book
2 doz. Cash's Name Tapes   (marked)
2 Hair Brushes and Combs
1 Sponge Bag
1 Sponge, Face Glove, Tooth and Nail Brush
1 Strong Bag for soiled linen
1 Rug
2 Pairs of Sheets
2 Pillow Cases
4 Table Napkins and Ring
4 Bath Towels   (2 not larger than 50 in. × 46 in.)
                (2 not larger than 44 in. × 22 in.)
1 Handbag, large enough to contain all requirements for
    the first night, about 16in. × 8in. × 8in.

3 Medium Grey Flannel Suits, with S
    last year, or unusually tall, may
    Sunday)
4 White Flannel Cricket Shirts   (c
2 Pairs of Grey Flannel Trousers
2 Pairs of Grey Socks
1 Pair of Brown Boots, studs f
    (These may be used in wir
1 Grey Soft Felt Hat
1 Pair of Red Stockings
*1 Blazer

Additional for Boys

2 Pairs of White Fla
1 Pair of White Bo
2 Pairs of White
2 (additional) W

3 Medium
2 "Rugg
3 Pairs
1 Pair
4 Cri

1

All School Caps, Stockings, Football Boots, Jerseys, Belt
* As these are uniform, it is preferred that they are b
    Westborough, Scarb

Dear Rod
Sept. 21st

BRAMCOTE,
SCARBOROUGH.
TEL. 828.

This is just to show I haven't forgotten you today as you are about to start a new career at Winchester. I hope you'll be v. happy as I am sure you will. With Michael and three others from here, things won't seem so strange to you as they might to some – and you'll soon get settled in. I met Dr. Jackson last Monday week as I was looking round Southwell Minster. He was staying with the Hams at Derby

53. Pidcock's letter to Roderick Cairns-Terry after he had gone up to Winchester. Roderick recalled: 'Pidcock's prayer at night was "Lord keep us safe this night secure from all our fears". On the last morning before we left he always used to say the 121st Psalm. And at the last service before leaving we always sang the 150th Psalm with the descant.'

...Cairns-Terry's clothes list.

Peter Gem (1935-39) wrote to *The Bramcotian* in 1988. He referred to Pidcock and Oswald Cooper as 'Pud' and 'Ozzie'. He explained that the masters had to do weekly day duty and in this way the boys got to know all of them:

On Monday, it was Mr Hamerton (Hammo), a Latin and Greek man and not one to be trifled with, but he was meticulously fair. He later became a headmaster of Bramcote. On Tuesday, Mr Stewart (Tubby), a fat little man who taught French in the more senior part of the school – and taught it well. He had what seemed to us very bizarre notions of nomenclature, insisting that we wore stockings (when of course we wore socks) and – of all things – knickers (when we wore shorts, except for the most senior boys on Sunday who were permitted 'longs'). On Wednesday, it was Mr Gamble who could be delightful but was often hard and horny-handed. He taught junior maths well, and was the driving force in more ways than one behind the soccer which was usually of a high order. He smoked Players cigarettes and boys were for ever going up to him to ask for cigarette cards; there used to be one in each packet of twenty.

On Thursday it was Mr Urling-Smith. He was an English expert and concentrated on style and grammar. He also had a scheme called 'Weekly Worders' when he gave out a list of the more unusual words and we had to use them in a sentence making it clear that we fully understood the meaning. We were issued with special little notebooks for this which he used to take in at the end of the week to correct. He was not a man to fool around with unless you fancied a painful session in the changing room on the receiving end of an epileptic gym shoe. Friday was The Day for me as this was presided over by Mr Baird (Sam). He was a quintessentially kind man and generally easy-going. Sam taught several subjects but his forte was English literature to Years 3 and 4. I should add at this point that the Forms then went 1, 2, Shell, 3, 4, Remove, 5. Sam's teaching of this subject remains one of the Everests of my school career both at Bramcote and Winchester. Although he spoke over our heads much of the time and at moments seemed almost to be communing with himself, those of us whom he reached became totally addicted and in some ways it is true to say that when I left Year 4, I then knew more about the generality of English literature than I did until I was very much an adult, and certainly far more than very nearly any boy now does when he leaves his Public School. Sam played the piano to us after prep in the evening on an old piano in the then library which was the room next to the big schoolroom. Saturday was another half holiday like Wednesday and it was on those days only that we were doled out a very few sweets. It seemed a terrible imposition then and the only way round it was to get three 'lists' and that entitled you to an extra hand-out of six sweets – usually on a Monday. Lists were published every Saturday when all the weekly marks for each subject were put up on the main board each on a separate sheet of paper. The boy who came top could claim the list at the end of that day and, if you got three, you took them along to either Pud or Ozzie and you got your reward.

Mr Hemming was a very able teacher of maths to the senior forms. It was to him that you went if you needed a new pen or some blotting paper; he always had a stock and kept the most meticulous account of what each of us had. He would also accept orders for toys which he would buy in town, for we were absolutely forbidden to go into town for anything except through the outskirts or to the harbour as part of an organised school walk. Most of the treasures that he brought back from these expeditions of his were, I think, Dinky toys, both cars and aeroplanes, beautifully made and selling at 6d or 9d – and for those not hot on antique money that means about 3p or 4p! (Others remember him bringing them foreign stamps for their stamp collections.) Saturday evening prep for the top two forms was always a maths test with ten questions each out of ten.

We had the occasional lecture as they were always called. One of the merits of these was that we missed prep. A heterogeneous collection descended on us informing us, *inter alia*, how they escaped from German prisoner of war camps in the First World War; how they had climbed a mountain – and this I greatly enjoyed, how someone or other had discovered some hideous fever swamp in Africa or Lancashire; talks with black- or to be precise grey-and-white slides on various aspects of architecture which again I enjoyed; and once, a conjuror who entertained us hugely especially when he muffed a trick and we gave him a most ungentlemanly derisory hoot.

54. Martin Stewart. 'I remember when an extra-cover drive for five, all runs, was struck to the furthest corner of the field off Mr Hamerton,' wrote Alick Wright (1922-27). 'I think "Tubby" Stewart, who was not the most nimble of men, had to run all the way to the edge of the field just short of the boundary. And he must have needed a relay of backers-up to get the ball back to the wicket! He did not wear any cricket club colours, but I remember that Mr Hamerton was a Sussex Martlet. Pidder looked even better in a "Butterflies" blazer and Ossie Cooper sported Oxford University authentic colours.'

55. Reading was a favourite pastime.

In the little spare time they had some boys worked on their stamp collections. There were magazines around to read, including those supplied by the school such as the *Illustrated London News*, *Punch* and a daily paper. 'The boys were encouraged to read and they used the library fairly well. Biggles was a great attraction in pre-war days,' Bevan Gamble said. Val Wrigley recalled they had a library stocked with such 'splendid writers for boys' as Stevenson, Buchan, Stanley Weyman and Conan Doyle. On Sundays Roderick Cairns-Terry remembered Pidcock reading the Father Brown stories with the boys sitting on desks in the main classroom, eating cakes topped with icing.

56. Peter Terry at Cayton Bay. When he retired as a school governor he was presented with a glass plate to commemorate his first 57 years' association with the school, 1927-84. He was a founder governor.

57. Peter Terry on the school climbing frame with Alfred Mather and Martin Phelps in 1932.

58. *Another hobby was making model aeroplanes. These little monoplanes with their wind-up elastic propellers were known as 'Frog Airplanes'.*

59. *And if all else failed there was drill on the playground.*

60. *The school buildings underwent another change in 1930 when the Changing Room and some classrooms were built between the Saverys' new house and Bramcote Lodge.*

61. *The school as it was around 1905 when Bramcote Lodge (centre) was initially linked to the new house. Netherbank is on the right.*

Triple D.S.O., Double D.F.C.—Face Of A Typhoon Ace

GREATEST OF ALL rocket Typhoon specialists, Group-Captain D. E. Gillam, D.S.O. and two Bars, D.F.C. and Bar, A.F.C., epitomises the nerveless daring of the tank and H.Q. busters on the Western Front. This magnificent study by Nurnberg is twelfth in our series, "The Fighting Face of Britain."—See Story on Page 2.

62. Top left: Dreaming of fast cars in August 1928 . . . Standing behind the car: Michael Munby and Christopher Foxley Norris. Seated in the car: Henry Gillam, John Foxley Norris and Michael Atter. Standing: Denys Gillam. Christopher Foxley Norris rose to the rank of Air Marshall and was knighted. Various stories are recounted about Denys Gillam's head for heights while at Bramcote.
63. Bottom Left: By February 18th, 1945 he was the talk of the country when the Sunday Graphic *featured him on their front page.*

Denys Gillam was one of the most decorated RAF pilots during the war. When he died the *Bramcotian* carried the following obituary:

'One of Bramcote's most distinguished old boys, Group Captain Denys Gillam, died in July 1991. He was born in Yorkshire and after leaving Bramcote he went to Wrekin College. He joined the RAF in 1935 and by 1940 was Flight Commander of 616 South Yorkshire squadron. He flew on operations in some of the first serious clashes with the Luftwaffe in 1940 and he fought throughout the Battle of Britain. In the remaining years of the war he led attacks on enemy shipping and ultimately became one of the RAF's finest exponents of ground attack in the campaign in North West Europe in 1944-45. His career was an extraordinarily long one given the mental and physical stress which sustained combat flying produces and his bravery was reflected in the fact that he was awarded a DSO with two bars, a DFC and bar and an AFC.'

After the war he returned to civilian life and was director of Homfray & Co. the family carpet firm. He was the Chairman between 1971 and 1981. He was active in public life and was Deputy Lieutenant of the West Riding of Yorkshire and of the City and County of York.

Another Bramcote boy who made a name for himself in the RAF during the war was Robert Irving (1922-26). He had gained a double first at Oxford and returned to Winchester as a music master, so when he joined the RAF he was nicknamed 'the flying symphony conductor'. In January 1943 he was awarded the DFC for his part in locating the *Scharnhorst*. Before he left the RAF at the end of the war he was asked to rewrite their navigation manual. Irving then spent three years as associate Conductor of the BBC Scottish Orchestra before moving to Covent Garden in 1949. In 1958 he was invited to become the Music Director of the New York City Ballet where he remained for over 30 years. He was also a keen bridge player, mountaineer and racehorse owner. He died in 1991.

CHAPTER 3

Disruption and Change
The Forties

Pidcock might well have retired before 1945 if the Second World War had not intervened. Even though Scarborough soon became 'home' to over 18,000 evacuees mainly from Hull[1] it was decided that the school should shift away from the coast. 'We were sent home a month early from the summer term 1940 so that Messrs Pidcock and Cooper could have time to find an alternative site,' wrote Michael Coates (headmaster 1968-69). 'I went to Bramcote in the summer term 1939, still four months before we were evacuated.' He continued:

My early memories are few and scattered: the problem of finding the lavatory on the first day, the godlike appearance of the older boys, the difficulty of securing my collar on unfamiliar studs, the vigour with which the matron dried my hair on bath nights, the crocodile to church, the relative fleeting comfort of Mrs Thomas's room when the Toads were invited in, and the Cayton Bay picnic, the freedom and fun of which seemed somehow out of keeping with the normal pattern of school life.

Just a few incidents stand out. One boy's unsuccessful attempt to commit suicide rather than face another of Mr Pidcock's Latin lessons; he ate some of the lime with which the groundsman marked the pitches, but apart from a frothing at the mouth it produced no ill-effect. The rebellion of a few enterprising souls who tired of the Head Boy's stately pace round the Mount on a Sunday afternoon walk and overtook him, followed by several of us younger children who knew no better – and my puzzlement that so reasonable and understandable an initiative should incur such awful displeasure. Awaking to the amusement of the other boys as matron carried me into the dug-out; I had slept through the air raid siren and been discovered absent from the roll call.

Many parents were in Scarborough for the Fathers' Match and Sports Day in June 1940 and were upset by the air raid warnings. Pidcock noted in the School Register:

At tea time on the Sports Day, they were asked to state their views whether they wished to stay or go. There were some fairly violent speeches on both sides – some of the 'go-ers' being a bit hysterical – and it would have appeared at first sight that a majority were ready to stay but on Sunday a small deputation arrived who said that although they wished to support us in every way, they would be happier if we moved. The fear of invasion undoubtedly played a large part in parents' minds.

Then followed a miserable month of searching for houses chiefly in Shropshire and the Lakes . . . Luckily news came through from Mrs Cooper's cousin that Eshton Hall,

[1] Dissertation by R.L. Feather *The Impact of the Second World War on Scarborough* p.29.

Gargrave in Craven, belonging to Sir Matthew Wilson Bart was available. Oswald Cooper, Mrs Cooper, Mrs Thomas and I saw the place and decided to take it. The house was naturally hideously inconvenient in various ways, particularly in the Matron's department, with shortage of bathrooms, sick room . . . The outside lavatories (four in number) were in a very poor condition.

'Eshton Hall was a terrific place for small boys to be let loose in,' said Richard Wilkinson (1944-49). 'There was a beck running through the grounds where we could dam it and sail motorboats and yachts.

'One of the major differences with the facilities in Scarborough was that Bramcote had, and still has, one of the best sports fields in the North of England. The 1st XI soccer field was an absolute beauty. Bramcote soccer was something very special. The boys were taught – and I am sure still are taught, precision football. At Eshton the football fields consisted of thick Pennine grass interspersed with cowpats, thistles and even animals. Frank Hamerton actually kicked a football at a cow to get it off the pitch so that we could get on with the game.'

'I was in both teams that won everything before the war,' mused John Cundall. 'We had to go to Eshton with a depleted school and had to play on that bad ground. I remember sitting after a match in the assembly room and being almost in tears because we had lost everything. Pidcock came and explained that you always get ups and downs in the standard of the school because of numbers etc. and no-one is blaming you. He did it in a terribly kind way. I have great memories of him being very kind to people.'

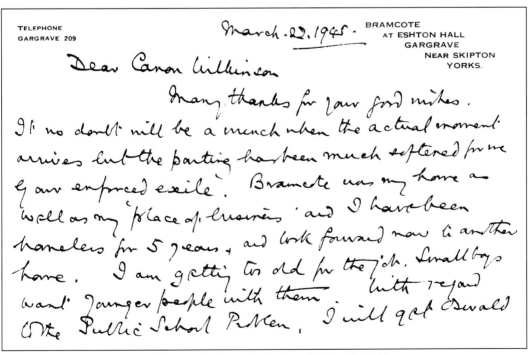

64. *Extract from a letter from Pidcock to the father of Richard Wilkinson.*

65. *Eshton Hall.*

For cricket they could practise on the lawns at Eshton, or they had to cycle to the cricket ground at Gargrave, as William Sager (1944-47) recalled:

'The smallest Toads played on the lawn between the south-western wall of the house and the road. Unofficial games and some catching practices took place in the rough grass on top of the bank at the back of the Hall. Every now and then the whole school went by bicycle to play on Gargrave village cricket ground. This seemed quite a ride and involved crossing the Leeds-Liverpool canal near a lock on the return journey. I liked these rides. There was also an annual ride to Winterburn Reservoir via Flasby and Hetton with a sort of picnic.' They went to Malham Tarn instead of Cayton Bay and went walking up Sharp Haw and Rough Haw. Sager added:

'In extremely wet weather it was "macs, caps and round the square" – a circuit of the Hall and Gardens – but every break – half an hour in the mornings – we had to go on the woodland walk circuit beside the beck, a very interesting and pretty walk. There was a generous walk to the church, doffing caps at Mrs Cooper who rented a house nearby. This was followed by a walk back, usually at a slow pace.' After a drink of newly boiled water (to make it less hard) they were off for another walk, with a third after lunch. These walks were usually along the road and they were seldom allowed to go on field paths. But those road walks had their moments of excitement as Coates recounted:

'Urling-Smith, indignant at the speed at which a car drove through our straggling walk, struck it with his walking stick as it went by and, to our delight, shouted "Don't drive like a bloody fool." The car came to a screeching halt and out of it got an enormous Yorkshire farmer. He approached Urling and shook his great fist in his face. "You keep yer pokes off me or I'll poke yer wiv one o' these." Urling coached the boxing, so we always assumed that he would have come off best. Mistakenly, as I now believe.' Urling-Smith, like the Berridge sisters and several others on the staff, had been with the school for many years and helped to provide a strong core, as Pidcock noted:

'We naturally, like everyone else, had great difficulties with domestic staff and at times our helpers included Czechs, Lithuanians and Russian Jews. The boys helped to wash up, sweep bedrooms, make their beds and clear meals. With regards to the teaching staff we were probably the most fortunate school in England. When war broke out the whole staff, bar one, had been here for eight years (or more) and were all over 30 and as schoolmasters were rejected by the authorities [for military service].' When the age was raised later Bevan Gamble and Roger Lace became eligible and they enlisted.

Wilkinson said he actually peaked in classics at the age of 14 because of Hamerton's efficiency. Coates pointed out that not only did the classics remain secure with Pidcock and Hamerton, but so did history with Cooper, English with Urling-Smith, maths with Hemming and French with Stewart, and music (such as it was) with Beedle. Otherwise, he said, there was a steady stream of 'temporary incompetents' who tried Pidcock and Cooper sorely. Sager and Wilkinson recalled that the bottom two forms were taught in the front hall and separated by screens which formed a passageway from the front doors to the inner hall. Mrs Mason often used one of these rooms.

'She lived locally and came in a black Standard 8, and taught French,' said

Sager. 'She was very nice, competent and most especially popular because she once came with a tray of home-made fudge which I can still visualise.' Wilkinson remembered however . . .

'Mrs Mason was not a great disciplinarian and one boy, who was a farmer's son, flatly refused to do something that Mrs Mason had told him to do. She then told him to get out and he said "No – I won't". Now, unfortunately for him, Oswald Cooper was teaching us on the other side of the partition and he descended on the poor boy like an avenging angel, shouting and spitting. In those days, of course, corporal punishment was the normal method of dealing with indiscipline or idleness . . . and Oswald was not a man to cross.' Coates remembered that too:

'A boy wrote an essay for Oswald Cooper on the Irish potato famine. His last word was – or should have been – "potatoes", but there wasn't room on the page. So, mindful of the need for wartime economy, he forbore to start a fresh page and wrote "spuds" instead. Oswald misinterpreted this as flippant insubordination and the anger of that normally patient and kindly man, as he flung not just the offending exercise book but all of them at the unfortunate culprit, was dreadful to behold.'

'Oswald was a wonderful teacher,' recounted Wilkinson. 'I thought he was a very, very good history teacher. And he certainly interested me. I can only emphasise my debt to him there as I teach history for a living myself' (at Marlborough, and he has recently completed a history text book on Louis XIV). He got to know Oswald Cooper particularly well as, under the dual-headmastership system he was one of Cooper's boys.

'I have always thought the world of him. He was basically a kind man and he was, I thought, absolutely fair. He had a temper but very rarely lost it – he was normally genial – and had, I think a very pleasant sense of humour. I remember once having the courage and the temerity (when swimming) to duck him and he took it in very good part and needless to say he pursued me across the pool and gave me a very thorough ducking indeed as punishment.

'And he was a good businessman. A favourite topic of conversation on walks was to work out how much profit the school was making. Because we knew what the fees were and we guessed what the staff were paid and how much the food cost (not much) and we estimated what the lighting and so on cost – all of these of course guesses by small boys and no doubt wildly inaccurate – but our conclusion was that the headmasters made a bomb.

'Oswald Cooper was once very angry with me. We had a rather absurd sad teacher called Potter who had been knocked about in World War One. He couldn't keep order and was a total figure of fun for us boys. Once – on some sports occasion – there was an egg and spoon race for staff and parents. The sight of old Potter competing caused me to double up with mirth. Ozzy saw this and absolutely rent me -"Who was this poisonous little boy to mock this elderly victim of modern war?" – that I suppose was Cooper's reasoning, and it did him credit.'

'However much impact the war made on our elders,' wrote Coates, 'it made little impression on us. Some of us learned to knit, so as to be able to knit khaki scarves . . . for the troops. I wonder who got mine; it was long, thin and full of unintended holes.'

Eshton Hall was a delight in summer with the sun streaming through the windows – but in winter it was another matter and the boys found it very hard to keep warm. Coates said they couldn't fathom Pidcock's fury when some boys innocently and unsuccessfully tried to keep warm by getting into each other's beds.

Rev. Martin Whitwell (1939-45) recalled that his god-father, Urling-Smith, used to read ghost stories to the boys in the dormitories which gave them a 'creepy and eerie' feeling. Wilkinson recalled:

'The dormitories were quite small – they were the bedrooms of the old family and needless to say it was firmly believed they were haunted and there were terrific ghost stories told about what happened after dark in Eshton. I think we rather enjoyed that. For three or four months of the winter at Eshton it was very dark and very ghostly – very dramatic and very romantic. Prep school boys always enjoy raiding other dormitories or raiding the sweet cupboard or whatever – and the whole exercise of raiding at Eshton was infinitely more exciting and easier than at Bramcote.'

The dormitories, however, were bitterly cold during the winter of 1944, according to Sager: 'There was much snow and once, by relays, we had to dig out the front drive by the gates and I think also most of the approach road. Once in a field opposite the Hall we had an afternoon making snowmen and then a snowball fight was organised. Twice we went sledging, once by the Dower House Farm and once in a field behind the wood alongside the beck. On the first occasion one chap and myself went slap into a barbed wire fence and both had to have stitches. There was one huge sledge called the Stage Coach which took six to eight boys.'

66. Pidcock used this picture in a Christmas card in 1941.

Nurses and Matrons

67. Nurse Jell 1911-14.

68. Miss Chaffer, Matron 1924-38.

69. Miss Stainton, Matron 1938-46.
'A formidable, unbending lady.' (John Cundall)

George Bagshawe believes he may well have good teeth today (at 91 years) because of the nurse at Bramcote. 'Nurse Jell was very particular about brushing your teeth and she checked on every boy in the junior school when you went to bed – she came into the bathroom and watched the boys clean their teeth. You were told you had jolly well got to brush them again if you hadn't brushed them enough. The other thing that was always inspected was the back of your neck – every boy had the back of his neck inspected by the matron as he was going to bed or when he was in bed. In that way we learnt to keep ourselves clean.'

The fear of constipation marked prep school life for decades and Peter Terry recalls that Miss Chaffer, faithfully fulfilled her duties . . .

'I think we used to get cascara once a week – cascara is a sort of laxative and it tasted ghastly, absolutely awful. And we used to have our ears examined every night by the matron or the assistant matron and we used to try and avoid going in to see her on the night it was cascara night.

'She was quite a martinet was Miss Chaffer – and if we did anything wrong and didn't comply with her instructions we got a ruler across the top of the hand which was quite sore.' John Cundall remembered she was not popular with the masters because she would let boys off games if they were only slightly ill.

But there were times when the matrons were up all night for sometimes weeks on end when epidemics struck the school. Whooping cough, scarlet fever, measles, mumps, and chicken pox (which even Oswald Cooper caught in 1925) regularly took their toll. In 1936 the School Register recorded that Jim Hornby was the first boy to come down with the German measles which 50 out of the 68 boys caught. It was probably due to the fear of epidemics that the small print on the bottom of their term reports read: 'It is particularly requested that boys should be kept away from Cinemas and cheap Public Entertainments during the fortnight preceding each term.'

In 1938 Easter Term began on January 21st. On February 3rd the first case of measles was diagnosed. All but two of the boys were innoculated on February 4th and 5th but by February 21st 44 had contracted the disease. The Sanatorium did not close till March 9th and six boys had to be sent home to convalesce. Only A.W. Ingleby and three boys who were absent did not catch the measles.

In the last weeks of Easter Term, the school was 'infected with some kind of influenza' and on Sunday March 20th Miss Chaffer was taken to the Belvedere Nursing Home with septic bronchitis and was in bed for almost eight weeks. As a consequence of her illness she resigned her post as Matron. Then, according to the School Register, 'On the evening of April 3 (Sunday) two days before the end of term Mrs Thomas (60th term) was taken ill and in two days time was seriously ill with pneumonia. From April 11th she began to get better, though very slowly.'

And in the Summer Term: 'A.W. Ingleby got scarlet fever; all the household had their throats swabbed with one 'positive', but we had no further cases. About the third week in the term one boy began a cough. This cough spread very mildly and during the first week in July was declared to be whooping cough, but no-one was ill and only about half a dozen in the sick room.' Nurse Stainton had replaced Miss Chaffer temporarily but then stayed on as Matron.

Sager remembered how Miss Stainton kept her headwear very well starched, and fed them on Radio Malt each week – a thick, sweet malt food supplement.

And as for the porridge they were fed on so regularly – she gave that to the red squirrels when at Eshton Hall.

In 1972 Tim Mansel and Dominic Robinson went to interview Frank Hamerton about the school's stay at Eshton Hall. He told them that the changing facilities at Gargrave were atrocious. The changing-room was a stone hut, with pegs to hang clothes on. There was no electrical heating, nowhere to dry clothes. The first Sunday at Gargrave, Frank Hamerton (then a master), not being familiar with the area, decided to take the boys up the road, cut across the moors and then come back by another road, thus making a triangle. Just as they were about to start across the moors, it started to rain. Frank Hamerton, thinking that rain would not harm the boys, decided to go on. Unfortunately the rain started pouring down, by which time they were halfway across the moors and climbing over innumerable walls. They eventually got back to Eshton Hall with all the boys soaked to the skin. To avoid the wrath of the matron, Frank Hamerton jumped onto his moped and rode quickly back home, to Skipton!

70. Some of those who did five years at Eshton. Back row: Frank Hamerton, a maid, Philip Beedle, Dot Berridge, the Assistant Matron Miss Kenworthy, A. Urling-Smith. Seated: Oswald Cooper, Elsie Berridge, Mrs Thomas, Walter Hemming, the Cook Miss Flo Berridge, Pidcock and the Matron Miss Stainton. On the ground: Neville Harris, Martin Whitwell, Michael Coates, Peter Wordie and John Dalling.

From 1944 Oswald Cooper took up writing the story in the School Register where he recorded the first moves to have the school derequisitioned from the Armed Forces. Both the Army and the RAF had used the grounds and buildings:

With the coming of 1945 things really began to move and finally it was decided that the school should be handed back on March 17th. As the Army had the playing fields we had to wait about a month longer before they also were returned. Then we had to start the Herculean task of restoring the whole place into working order. The School itself was not in bad condition. It was dirty and unkempt and a great many fixtures had been added when the place became a clinic which did a lot of damage to the walls when they were removed. They had also knocked a way into the gym from the schoolroom. The whole place had to be redecorated and a large number of repairs had to be carried out.

The field was entirely bare at the South end and the rest of it was rough and no attempt had been made to cut it for years. We decided to aim at coming back in September and made a start when I came back for the holidays in April. Every possible difficulty had to be overcome – getting cleaners, obtaining licences for repairs, materials, workmen, Government inefficiency etc. etc. When I returned to Eshton, Mrs Cooper kept things moving, but things looked pretty grim when I came back to Scarborough for good on July 26th. Urling-Smith and Hamerton saw about getting everything ready for moving at Eshton Hall and most competently they performed the task.

Meanwhile we wrestled at this end, and in August the stuff began to arrive and was dumped in the gym. Among our worst troubles was lino as we could not get the men to lay it, and we could not move stuff into any room until it was done. However, everyone worked unsparingly, and much to the astonishment of all spectators we were in fairly good shape to open on September 25th. We gained some extra days by giving the school an extra week-end instead of celebrating V.J. Day.

As to the field, it was first of all eaten down and from May to August we had 90 sheep, 30 cows and two horses grazing in it. They did well and all our neighbours delighted in the rural scene. After it had been cut and the white posts painted it looked more like its old self, though the rugger ground was still terrible and we did not use it in the January term.

Possibly it would have been wiser to have given ourselves another month to get the school ready as we were all very jaded and exhausted when term began.

Pidcock decided not to come back to Bramcote and retired to Winchester at the end of the Summer Term after being at Bramcote for 31 years. His partnership with myself had lasted 15 years. Urling-Smith and Hamerton joined me as partners but in June 1946 Urling-Smith got engaged to be married and decided to give up, so he retired at the end of the term.

There were many adjustments to be made with the departure of Pidcock, Mrs Thomas and Walter Hemming, the return of Bevan Gamble and Roger Lace, and the arrival of some new staff members.

These included Jim Hornby as Sager recalled: 'Hornby came for an interview in Naval uniform which greatly impressed some of us. He also produced a song which started with the upper parts of the body and descended as far as the stomach. Try as we could we never did find out the rest of the song!'

71. Mrs Thomas in 1928.

The Toads

'Toads? Not in my time,' commented George Bagshawe recalling the time he started in 1910. 'A new boy was known as a "new bug".' It wasn't until the mid-twenties that calling new boys 'Toads' became a feature of Bramcote life. The woman associated with the Toads, and who probably started calling them that, was Mrs Thomas who joined the school in 1918 as the housekeeper.

'Only the little ones went to Mrs Thomas' room. I remember her reading Dr Doolittle and the animals,' said Val Wrigley who was at Bramcote 1924-29. When John Cundall started school in 1935 he recalled:

'The Toads didn't do prep at nights. She used to take them down to her private quarters and she would read to them. In the room she had a realistic brass toad three to four times bigger than usual.' He did not know, however, whether she got the toad because the youngest ones were already called Toads, or if the name was associated with her having this brass ornament. One suggestion was that, as her room was so small, the boys had to squat on the floor to all fit in – and that reminded her of toads. But who knows?

At Eshton Hall she took over Lady Wilson's furnished drawing room to have her Toads gatherings. 'She would often just chat to us, comfort us and sometimes read. She seemed kindly,' remembered William Sager. When Mrs Thomas left in 1945 the new housekeeper was Miss Aston.

'Miss Aston was a large motherly woman whom I remember better for her extreme kindness to the Toads, providing games in her own quarters in the evenings and teaching the illiterate ones to read and write on a one-to-one basis during the day,' recalled Dr Stewart Morison.

In 1987, Nicholas Clark (then aged eight) wrote: 'It is fun to be a Toad. The Toads get extra things like films, and sweets for good work. When the seniors have prep the Toads have Toad time (time when we do fun things). On Saturday night we have a film with Mrs Wilson.' In the same *Bramcotian* it was reported that Mrs 'Bobby' Wilson was leaving and observed:

'Nobody entering Bobby's room at Bramcote could have been in any doubt where her heart lay: she must have the largest collection of Toads in the country. For the last three years our Toads have been very much the centre of her life. Whether in the Toads' art room upstairs, or in her room watching a film with the young, or on Sunday walks or games of rounders, Bobby has given unstintingly of her time. All the while she has fulfilled all the usual matronly duties with great efficiency.'

For it is now the Matron and her staff who have special responsibility for the Toads. They put them to bed and get them up, and take care of them on Sundays. Others, including Mary Gerrard and Juliet Moyle, have also spent a lot of time with the Toads, like the soft toy making sessions by the fire in the Gerrard's home during the 1980s.

72. *Mrs Thomas at the Toads' Feast around 1932.*

73. *The new Toads with their 'fathers' in 1983. In the 1970s each Toad was linked up with a slightly older boy who was termed his 'father'. The 'fathers' are in school uniform.*

74. Hemming (standing on left) with Savery (seated centre) in 1909.

75. Hemming just before he retired – and still wearing the same style of collar.

Reminiscences of Dr Stewart R. Morison (1947-53)

My arrival at Bramcote in 1947 was instantly a happy one – the war was won, the Empire still a matter of pride, and most of the staff were 'war heroes' in one way or another. Britain was still great and this national pride was shared by staff and pupils alike.

The excitement of sleeping in a dormitory with other boys to whom I could talk (although we were not meant to!) was only marred by one boy who was desperately homesick and whose tears spoiled our conversations!

'Ossie' Cooper (a great headmaster), whose 4th and 5th right-hand fingers had been 'blown-off' by a shrapnel of shell at Gallipoli – he claimed the noise woke him up, but he felt no pain! – still insisted in shaking hands with all new boys, and this was slightly unnerving to a boy of eight, but gave us strength to accept his own acceptance of his disability which appeared nothing to him. His lovely wife was a tower of strength for Bramcote, almost always round the school, until she was sadly afflicted with what I can now only assess as Multiple Sclerosis, ending up in a wheelchair.

Frank Hamerton kept himself very much in the background as far as we boys were concerned but he had two fantastic assets as far as they affected us:

He had – even in the sight of us young boys – an absolutely gorgeous looking wife[1], who was rarely seen on school premises, but as they lived in a house just beyond the end of the playing-field, I am ashamed to confess that we used to watch her through a telescope from school, rather in the way of some Hitchcock thriller!

As a teacher, he was probably without equal in my life. Without any pressure that I can remember, I was translating Leaders from *The Times* into Latin verse at the age of 11-12. Both headmasters were Oxbridge graduates, as were all the other teachers, with the possible exception of Miss Bolton, and these were as follows:

Jim Hornby, a typical Winchester scholar, including the permanently blocked nose they all seem to have, who had been something of a 'star' in the D-Day landings apparently. Sandy Stow, another war hero with a bullet still in his leg, which had withered, forcing him to wear a caliper, which gave his walk a most distinctive 'dum-de-dum' noise, although he could and did still run like the wind. Sandy finally managed to teach me to swim in the big outdoor pool in Scarborough and later saved my life when I developed a severe cramp whilst swimming across the deep end under the diving board.

Roger 'Squeaky' Lace, an RAF hero, complete with moustache (and leather flying jacket, noted James Archer), who was very popular with the boys, as he was always heard coming from a distance wearing crepe-soled shoes which squeaked on the school floors, hence the nickname!

'Fraz' Fraser – an absolute TYRANT of a man – we dreaded Fridays, when he was 'on duty'. In spite of which comments, he was universally accepted for his real talents as a teacher of maths (I still use his methods of algebra and trigonometry). As the true artist that he was, he always decorated the sets for the school plays and ran the films on Saturdays, which were always brilliant.

---

[1] Hamerton had married the sister of Seymour Baird, who was a master at the school until he became a partner at Lisvane School.

Philip Beedle was our piano teacher and choirmaster – a hyperactive little man with a very bald head, he appointed me as head chorister, I suspect because I was the only one who could hit top 'E'! A nice man. All the above lived in or around the school premises, the exception being . . .

Bevan Gamble who lived half-way up Oliver's Mount, but who was such a fit, loose-limbed individual and a great football coach that I suspect he was able to get into school sooner than some of the others! I can still hold my own against my children re Capital Cities, Rivers and even Countries! I am indeed dismayed by the modern generation's ignorance of our world.

'Cook' Berridge who knew everyone by their first name (but) I don't think anyone, even Mrs Cooper, knew her name! A formidable dragon of a woman, whose kitchen was her shrine. Her diet was totally repetitively predictable, day by day, week by week, and nothing would persuade her to let us have any variation on her theme!

After 'lights-out', there was absolutely no lighting on the stairs or corridors within most of the school. At this time, I was in dormitory nine, a four-bedded attic of a room above Matron's Office. In the night, I needed a 'pee' and groped my way down to the nearest toilet, two floors below. I then had to grope my way up again, and on arriving at the door I thought was my dormitory, I opened it and walked straight in, expecting to find my bed with no problem. In the total darkness I had picked the wrong door and was surprised to find myself falling into 'space'! I had walked into Cook's bedroom, which had two or three steps down into it. Luckily I was not hurt in any way, but I still don't know who was more frightened by this intrusion – Cook, resplendent in long nightgown, curlers and nightcap or myself (who I would guess by now was a ten year old boy).

There was a room beneath Frank Hamerton's study, euphemistically known as 'the games room' when I first went to Bramcote. In fact it was a cold, bare room, almost 'out-of-bounds' to us, but to my young mind it offered many possibilities, containing as it did a cupboard in which were an electric train set and various other goodies of interest.

The banks around the playing fields, and the hedgerows along the main marvellous school walks, were teeming in those days with a profusion of plants and insects – I particularly remember the Burnet moths which would sit for hours on my lapel and the soldier beetles. But it took me a long time for my newly acquired interest in lepidoptera to be accepted, although finally it was, and I was allowed to have containers of various species of caterpillars in 'the games room'; following which other boys could hardly be refused access, and the train was brought out and well used thereafter.

There was an old mantle-clock in this room, which hadn't worked for years. I took it apart and tried to make it go, but without success. My younger brother, Brian, joined Bramcote in my last year – by which time 'the games room' was flourishing – and he took that clock apart, put it together with two bits left over, and it kept perfect time thereafter! The reason for mentioning this at all, is that although Brian went on to obtain an Honours Degree in Archaeology, he is working as the main restorer of antique clocks in the North of England! That old Bramcote clock, in a room which I fought to 're-open', started it all!

Bramcote – a Fleeting Glimpse

by Peter J. Blayney (1949-54)

In 1949 there was food rationing and the Bramcote toad could scarcely survive on what was available from housekeeper-extraordinary, the redoubtable Miss Aston. So '*Agimus tibi gratias, Omnipotens Deus . . .*'[1] and survival became a preoccupying DIY task.

Many cunning and not-so-cunning ways were found of supplementing the diet of boiled rabbit, polony sausage, marmite on toast, fish on Friday and, for breakfast, scrambled egg resembling runny porridge or was it the other way round? Hairbrush lockers of the resourceful concealed tin lids containing soggy blotting paper on which struggled meagre strands of yellow mustard and cress. In the summer, digging for victory took on a new form. Gastronomic bliss was assured with a patch of earth from round the perimeter of the playing field which, with miraculously acquired horticultural zeal, would yield succulent radishes, promising carrots, novice lettuces and of course luscious green mustard and cress. True, gardens were really for flowers, but under the austere regime prevailing, a blind eye was turned though, as a gesture, nasturtiums were grown; but these too were eaten. How well Lacey guarded his strawberries! The Cayton Bay picnic became not a care-free outing to the beach, but a rare sea-food forage. Cauldrons of shrimps[2] skilfully caught by hand, were brought back triumphantly to be eagerly consumed that very evening. Exeats (leave-outs), anticipated for weeks, were spent not in the revitalisation of parental bonds but in orgies of fish and chipped potato, high teas with lashings of bread and butter and ice-cream sundaes at The Villa Esplanade. Sunday walks could yield tasty cliff-top blackberries in season. Tales reached eager ears of delicious away-match teas – Aysgarth stew and dumplings topped the bill. One resolved, therefore, to excel at sport. Enterprising ways were devised of depriving one's fellow of the contents of the tins of sweets issued twice weekly by Matron Kenworthy. Long queues formed for Radio Malt and for anything else worth consuming. Nurse Smith was a sure touch for the cough mixture, but contact with 'Dr Tommy' was to be avoided at all costs, for his cure for everything from the stubborn boil to the mumps was 'starvation'. So one learned to compromise on one's ailments and the stiff upper lip prevailed as did the mandatory cold bath, ' . . . if it was good enough for Hornby . . . besides we were shelled in the first war and survived.'

What dimensions were expressed, endeavours made and lessons learned! Thus grew the boy in the King's reign '. . . *pro his et universis donis tuis.*'

[1] First line of the 'after meat' grace.

[2] Such quantities can no longer be caught due to pollution.

James Archer, who joined the school in 1947, remembered:

Term started on York Station where the majority of the boys caught the steam train to Scarborough. There were no corridors, and each compartment had, either side of a mirror, pictures of holiday resorts from around the British Isles, almost all accessible by train. The carriages were sturdily made of teak wood, and the compartments were decorated each in different hardwoods, such as amboyna or keroin, imported from the far flung corners of the British Empire. In 1946 the line was run by the LNER Company with its Light Green livery, and teak coloured coaches. A large number of the engines were still in their wartime colour of plain black. But by 1947 the Socialist post war Government had nationalised the railways, and the coaches changed eventually to Plum and Spilled Milk.

The trip home at the end of term was also by train, the boys being collected by bus and taken to Scarborough Station. The bus ride was always one of the highlights of the term, and was noted for its sing-song. A tradition of the leavers was to throw their school caps into the Ouse at York, as they passed over the bridge and drew into the Station. This practice was frowned upon by the School Authorities, as they said that poor people from York would pick up the caps, wear them, and bring the school into disrepute.

Oswald Cooper had an old Lanchester car, which was more often than not parked on the Filey Road, outside the school. As a little boy it seemed very old to me, as its windscreen was yellow with age, the celluloid having weathered within the triplex screen. It was a car ahead of its time, being an automatic, rare in those days.

The Mecca of most boys (on Sunday leave-outs), that is those who lived any distance away, was the Villa Esplanade, with its beans on toast and icecream sundaes. My parents stayed in the early days at the Pavilion Hotel, just across the road from the Railway Station. It was typical of all the Grand Hotels in the last days of the Empire, with its Trio playing light classical music, and little old ladies taking afternoon tea in the spacious lounge.

Scarborough was different too. In the season the harbour and, to a lesser extent the bay was full of drifters following the shoals of herring down the East Coast. These were not the sleek low-slung models of today, but the last of the steam boats with their long thin rusty smoke-stacks and russet gaff rigged sails. Now there are no ships, or herrings: the former seeking richer pastures, as the latter have been fished to the point of extinction with the help of increasingly efficient technology. I remember vividly the winter of 1947 with its desperate cold. It is the only time in my life that I have had chilblains on my knees as well as my toes.

Oswald Cooper was the real headmaster, with a very highly polished bald head. He ran the school with a rod of iron, and was much respected by boys and parents. My most vivid memory of him is when he was blown up on Guy Fawkes Night. Unlike now, the parents formed a square round the playground, and most of the fireworks seemed to go inwards. The fireworks were much more dangerous too. There were jumping crackers, thunderflashes, and aeroplanes. In fact when underway it was like the battle of the Somme. Cooper used to stand by the bonfire, wreathed in smoke, as Master of Ceremonies. That year an aeroplane flew into his pocket and blew an enormous patch out of his coat. He looked more like the guy who had fallen from the fire. Poor chap!

However he shook it off as if nothing had happened, and mayhem continued. How nobody was ever killed or seriously hurt I will never know.

'Swimming started in the gym,' Sager wrote. 'Balanced somehow on benches we went through the motions of the various strokes. Originally, on returning to Scarborough, two or three times in the summer a bus was hired to take us to the heated Peasholm Bath (although it was an open air one). The next year we braved the cold of the South Bay Pool for which our daily cold baths should have inured us.'

'When the water was about 56 degrees,' Bevan Gamble said, 'we stood in water up to our chests to instruct children. It wasn't very pleasant and we had to revive ourselves with rum afterwards. Of the new boys who came in September nearly all could swim by the end of their first summer term. Everyone helped with instruction except Martin Stewart.' Urling-Smith made quite a reputation for himself at diving.

Boys at Bramcote in the 1950s also remembered. 'We weren't allowed to jump off the high board – I think it was 32ft. high,' said Stephen Hollins-Gibson. 'We were allowed to jump off the table and the platform above it which was great fun.' The table was called the bread board and the platform above, the cheese board.

76. *Bevan Gamble (in swimming suit), Frank Hamerton and Oswald Cooper organising a diving competition at the South Bay Pool about 1947.*

Bramcote and St Martin's, South Cliff

When the school evacuated to Eshton the Vicar of St Martin's, Rev. H. Spence, held a special service in June 1940, entitled 'A Reminder of Sunday Mornings in St Martin's'. In this he told the school:

'Ever since I came to St Martin's as vicar seven years ago, I have received loyal support and constant friendship from the owners and headmasters of the school, from the staff and the boys, and from everyone associated with it. The privilege of teaching in the school every week in term time has been one of the happiest features of my work here.'

One of the earliest vicars from St Martin's to teach divinity and take confirmation classes at the school was Hugh Tapper's father (1918-23).

Bramcote's connection with St Martin's began with Savery in whose memory there is a plaque at the Church. When Savery died it was noted at his memorial service: 'He saw clearly . . . the vital importance of publicly witnessing every Sunday to his belief in the ideals of the Christian faith.'

The long crocodile of boys wending their way to matins each Sunday became a feature of life in South Cliff and was recommenced after the war. But by then Rev. H.Spence had left and his place was taken by Rev. Windley. Sager remembers twice winning a prize from Rev. Windley for his annual Scripture test. Dr Morison wrote:

'Rev. Windley was also a war victim, with only a stump left of his right upper arm, which he used to wedge his books under and would wave around furiously when giving a sermon.' In fact, according to Sager, on one occasion Rev. Windley became so animated that he almost fell out of the pulpit. Yet, for all that, Dr Morison felt that a quite brilliant lecture on *Pilgrims Progress* given on one occasion at the school and accompanied by many very beautiful slides, was much more of a religious experience than some services. Richard Wilkinson said:

'Bramcote then aimed at Christianity based on knowledge of the Bible and two sermons every Sunday and a service every day. Oswald was, I think, a very devout and very good evangelical Christian. We all had to go to St Martin's every Sunday – rather surprising in a way because St Martin's was High Church, but it was the nearest.

'Visitors must have been very impressed by these scrubbed and polished immaculately behaved little boys and particularly they would have been impressed by our public spiritedness when the collection took place because the bag would go round and every boy would contribute. Perhaps they did not suspect that before we went down to church we were all issued with a silver threepenny bit which we then had to put in the bag. And then if the number of threepenny bits collected did not tally all hell was let loose.' Yet it was on these walks to church that the boys found that even the dreaded Fraser had a soft spot, as Mike Kitching and his friends realised.

'The big dare on the walk was to distract the master and someone would nip off and buy an icecream (with their threepence). Fraser never deemed that a mortal sin – that was part of the game.'   The boys then, however, did not have the same temptations as faced by those in Bagshawe's days. Queen Margaret's was still just off Filey Road, and there was another girls' independent school nearby. The girls walked down one side of the Filey Road, with the Bramcote crocodile on the

77. Sketch of St Martin's church on the front cover of the small booklet printed for the special service in June, 1940.

other, the boys all looking like perfect gentlemen in their Eton suits and top hats. 'Anybody who whistled got into serious trouble,' he chuckled.

The school's conception of itself as being Christian and how this affected the development of the 'whole boy' had a major impact over the decades. In the 1970s and 1980s it influenced views on corporal punishment and how to enable each boy to grow with dignity and self respect. For one of the boys, Henry Standing in 1990, some of this was expressed in his rendering of Psalm 23:

> The Lord (God) guides me so that I have everything I need.
> He helps me to sleep quietly and peacefully
> throughout the night and helps me to keep calm.
> He has helped me to understand that He can forgive the mistakes I make and
> has led me in a moral and civilised manner.
> When I die I will have no fear of hell because I know that God's
> protection is with me.
> While He gives me everything and treats me like a prince He gives nothing
> to people who are my enemies.
> Forgiveness and goodness will be with me as long as I keep faith in God
> and I will live in paradise forever.

When St Martin's replaced matins with Communion on Sunday mornings Bramcote started to hold its own weekly service at the school in which the vicar of St Martin's often participates. Nowadays the long crocodile snakes down the road to church only twice a term. And in anoraks instead of macs!

Looking Towards the Fifties

'Oswald Cooper never wanted the school to go over a hundred,' Peter Terry commented. 'He wanted to know each one and be able to write a letter about them every term. But Oswald Cooper and Pidcock were diehard conservatives who didn't want to see a good school change.' On trying to describe that era now Richard Wilkinson initially referred to it as 'horrendously masculine' but later wrote:

'My wife suggests that the word "austere" sums up the Bramcote atmosphere of 45 years ago, which is I think a fair comment. Of course they were austere times! But the whole ethos of the place – rigorous competition, no mercy for the unsuccessful, work hard, play hard – was Spartan. Perhaps Prussian is a better word, as intellectual/academic standards certainly existed.

'One point I would like to stress – there was kindness at Bramcote, even in my first traumatic term at Eshton. Kenworthy, the assistant Matron, and dear Philip Beedle both helped me to get through to Christmas. And throughout my time there, there was much friendship among my contemporaries and many productive staff-pupil relationships. Bramcote taught us to listen to adults with curiosity and appreciation. This was rather unusual.'

Pidcock, whose name was now so synonymous with the school that some believed he had actually founded it, returned in November 1946 when the parents and Old Boys made a presentation to him. Presentations were also made to Walter Hemming and Mrs Thomas who were retiring after serving the School most devotedly for 41 and 27 years respectively. According to Bevan Gamble Mrs Thomas then went to work as Mr Pidcock's housekeeper in Winchester. Sager reported that Mrs Cooper, who was definitely the Queen Bee at the school after the War, briefly acted as housekeeper but not too successfully.

Roderick Cairns-Terry met Pidcock at a match at Winchester after his retirement. 'He came up to me and put his arm around me. It was after the war and I suppose he had lost so many and was so glad to see someone who had survived.'

In his retirement Pidcock's activities included being the Honorary Secretary of the Mid-Hants Moral Welfare Association and helping in the State Education Scheme as a Manager of both All Saints School and Holy Trinity School, Winchester. He was taken ill in early 1952 and died on July 31st. *The Hampshire Chronicle* referred to him as the headmaster of 'one of the most outstanding preparatory schools in the north of England'. Jim Hornby wrote as an obituary:

In a world where individuality and character are in danger of being smothered and where true leadership is all too rare, 'Pidder' will be sadly missed; few men can ever have visualised their purpose in life more clearly or carried that purpose through more effectively. At Bramcote he was beloved by his staff and honoured and respected by all: to him the school was his life and almost to a fault he devoted himself to its well-being. To us, as boys, he was fearful yet never unapproachable, irascible yet never unsympathetic; severe yet always kind. He had an astonishing memory for people and faces and his letters, always written in his own beautiful, scholarly hand, were works of art. He was a most zealous follower of sport and when Bramcote was evacuated during the 1939-45 war he developed a love for the simple beauty and pleasures of a country life which he himself admitted he had never appreciated before. His last years were spent in retirement at

Winchester, the place which above all others was nearest to his heart; there, in his garden, in his frequent visits to the school, in his many friends, and in his new interests he found supreme happiness.

Peter Gem wrote to Oswald Cooper after the funeral: 'With the usual conceit of an ex-pupil I fear I may have slightly nonplussed you at St Cross today. The truth was that you had changed not a jot, and I forgot temporarily that I had grown up a little since 1939. It was however delightful to see you again even though, as you said, the occasion was such a very sad one. Especially for you, the loss must have been severe having worked so long together in such a cause. To so many of us who had the honour – not too strong a word – to be at Bramcote in the aegis of you two, it is a sorrow to know that the great partnership has been finally broken.'

78. *Oswald Cooper and Richard Pidcock in 1931.*

CHAPTER 4

Setting the Foundations of Change
1950–1969

The school flourished in this period with the number of boys reaching a plateau of around 85 to 95 boys and then rising above 100 for the first time in 1968. There was a steady stream of scholarships, including James Sabben-Clare's achievement of first place on the Winchester Election Roll.

In the early 1950s Oswald Cooper was considering retirement and originally expected that he would sell the school to a new dual-headmaster team. Jim Hornby (1932-37) had already helped out for a while in 1946 before going to Oxford and Oswald Cooper asked him to find one other to return with him to Bramcote. So, in 1954, Sandy Stow accompanied Jim Hornby from Oxford. Sandy Stow, however, left Bramcote a year later to join his family's preparatory school of Horris Hill.

The future of Bramcote when Cooper retired became something of a problem, and eventually the school was transferred on April 5th 1957 to a company limited by guarantee and registered as a charitable trust which was formed for the purpose of continuing the school. The necessary funds were provided by generous donations and covenanted subscriptions to the Trust from those close to the school; it was not necessary to launch a general appeal for funds. Cooper became Chairman of the Governors of the Trust and the Governors appointed Frank Hamerton and Jim Hornby to be headmasters. Cooper was joint headmaster until he retired at the end of the Summer Term that year.

Douglas Campbell (whose son Robert was then at the school) was one of the school's greatest benefactors at that time. Campbell made a considerable loan towards the cost of buying out Oswald Cooper, who owned the fabric of the school and he bought the two staff houses in Holbeck Avenue. He was a Governor from 1957 till 1977. In an obituary in the 1991 *Bramcotian* it was stated: 'There is no doubt that the strong financial position that the school holds today is due to his help and guidance.' His own solicitor, Geoffrey Hickman, who gave so much assistance with setting up the Trust, was invited onto the Board and remained a Governor for 27 years. The school faced many changes in this period – changes that Oswald Cooper often found difficult, according to John Cundall who joined the Board of Governors in 1968. He said that one of the original Governors, E.E. Sabben-Clare (father of James), proved especially helpful and influential for he had been headmaster of Leeds Grammar School. The strengths and weaknesses of the school were well documented in a report by HM Inspectors of Schools in early 1948.

In this report the inspectors noted that the staff were adequately qualified for the work they were expected to do, and their relationship with the boys, though on occasions pontifical, was pleasant and companionable and that a family atmosphere prevailed. The boys were well fed and cared for but the school day was a long one and was largely devoted to organised activity either in work or play. 'It would be an advantage if the boys could have a little more free time for unorganised and unsupervised hobbies, and quiet occupations, such as reading', they stated and made the following points about the school:

> The classrooms are all adequate for the small forms into which the school is divided: many of the desks are, however, so old fashioned and badly designed as to be quite unsuitable. There is also a marked lack of good pictures and illustrative material in general. The lay-out of the Curriculum reflects clearly enough the over-riding concern of the authorities of the school to obtain good results in the Common Entrance and Public Schools Scholarship Examinations and it must be said at once and without reservation that the results actually achieved in these examinations are outstandingly good. At the same time, the Curriculum is an extremely narrow one and ill-suited to the wider needs of boys of the 8 to 13 age group.'

The inspectors especially referred to the absence of systematic teaching through the school of art, music, manual training and elementary general science; the entirely artificial division of the English teaching into periods variously labelled 'English', 'Recitation', 'Copying', 'Reading', 'Spelling' etc. In their conclusions on curriculum they stated:

> The general impression obtained was that of a school in which early and continued concentration on a fixed objective leads to the acquisition of high, if somewhat mechanical, standards of achievement in certain narrowly defined fields of study. [The school] continues to do some excellent work and its reputation among schools of its kind is justifiably high. Nevertheless the Curriculum is narrow, according to present day conceptions of the needs of boys of Preparatory School age and some of the teaching techniques still in use are now obsolete. Its continued success, however, seems assured – so assured in fact that some degree of experiment . . . could be embarked upon without endangering either its standards or its traditions.'

This was to be the crucial factor as the school moved towards the 1970s. The constant concern was how to change without losing its academic standards or its strong, vibrant traditions, like the yearly picnic at Cayton Bay or the school's links with St Martin's Church. The boys continued every week to walk in a long crocodile to attend Sunday matins throughout the 1950s and 1960s. Colin McGarrigle (1949-54), who was headmaster from 1968 until 1983, said that both Oswald Cooper and Jim Hornby had close links with the Anglican church and were very committed to traditional forms of worship. This made it especially difficult for them to consider changing the Sunday routine. Alternative forms of worship for the evening services were considered but the links with St Martin's were firmly retained.

Colin McGarrigle saw Jim Hornby's time as very significant in the school's evolution and explained when interviewed: 'Jim Hornby introduced more lectures, he was a bit more global. Oswald Cooper was so narrow. He didn't see the need for anything else if you got four-five scholarships or so every year because of learning Latin verse. I didn't do any science, at prep or public school. I just did Latin. So the early stages of gentle modernisation began with Jim Hornby. But it takes time to change – both at parental and staff level. Frank Hamerton was still wanting the school to be the old Bramcote he knew from Eshton days – and Bevan Gamble had his doubts about change too. So you still had these older influences.'

'Hamerton very much clung to the traditions of the Cooper/Pidcock period but gradually changes took place,' John Cundall said. Yet even those who speak out forcefully against various aspects of this period, like Freddy Markham, felt they gained a lot too from being a schoolboy there. He, like many others, pointed to the amount of memory learning they had to do which left them with a hidden reservoir of geography and history information and a deep love of poetry. And he remarked: 'Jim Hornby was a man of the greatest integrity. I think we learnt the highest moral standards there and although one cannot say one always lived up to them afterwards, one always knew what they were and recognised them as being good and that the world needs them.'

Jim Hornby developed close links with the Incorporated Association of Preparatory Schools (IAPS) and, in 1966, became only the second member from the North to be elected its Chairman. His involvement with the IAPS over the years made him more aware of the changes occurring in education. One of his biggest innovations was to re-introduce science into the school curriculum (Savery had included it) and by 1963 a new science room was constructed. Bramcote was, in fact, one of the first prep schools to have a science laboratory.

Jim Hornby also took on the job of raising £30,000 through an Appeal to old boys and friends so that a new assembly hall could be constructed and thus release the gym for its real purpose. The only space available was the garden between Netherbank and Bramcote and by 1965 the shape of the school had undergone a fundamental change. The new hall was dedicated by the Archbishop of York in March 1965. Above the hall were a music room, art room and another classroom – clear signs that further changes were underway.

In July 1967 Jim Hornby left Bramcote to become headmaster of Clifton College Preparatory School. Michael Coates (1939-45) was appointed as his successor and Hamerton agreed to stay on for one further year 'to see him in'. On his retirement in 1968 Hamerton said he had seen a tremendous growth in teaching techniques, including a decline in the emphasis on his subject (the classics) relative to maths and science. Colin McGarrigle then joined Coates as assistant headmaster. 'Michael Coates wanted change,' commented Colin McGarrigle – but those were difficult years in many ways. It was a transitional period as regards staff (often due to retirement) and fundamental changes in the syllabus did not make things any easier. Michael Coates moved on to Monkton Combe Junior School, resigning from Bramcote in November 1968, having prepared the way, Colin McGarrigle said, for him to begin an era of major changes.

79. *Above: G.G. Hiscocks teaching in the new science laboratory.*
80. *Below: The plans for the Hall, linking Netherbank to the School. Until that time the single masters were accommodated at Netherbank. Before the hall was built Oswald Cooper had referred to the school's buildings as being 'a masterpiece of improvisation'.*

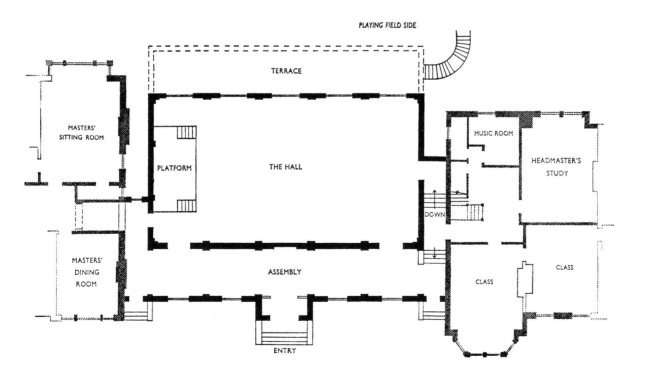

Looking Back on the 1950s:

Mike Kitching left Bramcote in 1950. One memory he especially cherishes is his friendship with the Coopers. He described Oswald Cooper as a tall, impressive man and went on:

'He was the dominant influence in the school then who set the standards of integrity. I was never frightened of him. He did beat the boys – with a cane. You were intensely proud of course. You had to go and show your stripes to your colleagues. But he was completely and absolutely fair and never raised his voice. I remember him as a very kind man. His wife Beatrice was the ideal headmaster's wife, a huge bundle of love and affection. She seemed to busy herself most with the youngest ones – the Toads. And she was the one who had those in the play for special tea. It was always Shakespeare. Fraser produced it and the celebration tea was a great privilege for those taking part.'

Fraser gave them an excellent grounding in maths, he said, but most of the boys feared him. 'Fraser was constantly losing his temper,' Kitching recalled. 'At Netherbank I think they had a barrel of beer and some small boy let the cork out. I remember him ranting and roaring about that.'

Only the older boys could take part in the sock fights – something which had started before his time and which were run on military lines by the masters two or three times a year. Blackboards and desks were upturned to make barriers running down two sides of the gym. With the masters as umpires two teams hurled socks at each other. When hit a boy had to retire. The team with the last remaining boy won. 'It was hugely exciting,' he said.

A particularly memorable event was visiting Oliver's Mount when motor bike races were held there – and the tremendous excitement of sitting on a bank and watching the fast motor bikes roaring past. On another occasion they were taken into Scarborough to watch an American heavyweight training for a fight. But it was the wonderful freedom in his last year to be among those who slept at Oswald Cooper's house, Willersley (across the Filey Road), that Kitching appreciated most.

'We always had a cup of cocoa with Mrs Cooper and Betty (her daughter) before bed. We saw a lot of the family. Betty was working on a farm up in the hills. I remember Sunday afternoons in the garden with the tortoises and the great love Beatrice Cooper had for all of us.'

The Cooper family, from 1949, took in the overflow from the school for a few years and as Kitching commented: 'It was considered a huge privilege.' He, like some other boys, returned in the holidays and stayed with the Coopers and went with them to the Scarborough Cricket Festival. Gradually Mrs Cooper became more and more bound to a wheelchair and one of the groundsmen, Joe Ward, used to carry her up and down stairs. He also used to drive for the Coopers.

81. Top Right – The rugby 1st XV in 1954. Standing: Christopher Browne, Denis Fearnley, James Sabben-Clare, John Butler, Richard Crombie, Thomas Russell. Seated: Richard Blachford, Colin McGarrigle, George Waller, Peter Blayney, Edward Hossell. On the ground: Peter Wright, Mark Bain, Michael Payne, and Victor Horsfall Turner.

1954

Bramcote v. Aysgarth, March 1954: Bramcote won by two goals, one penalty goal and four tries. 'We had not long to wait for a score, as in the third minute McGarrigle made the first of his many breaks and was stopped only inches short of the line. A quick heel from the ensuing ruck gave Sabben-Clare his chance and he dived over the line, McGarrigle converting. Then we saw the beginning of the domination of our forwards . . .' And so it was recorded in the School Match Book as had been every match (rugby, football and cricket) and every sports day since Slater and Pidcock took over the sports at Bramcote. (This practice continued until about ten years ago.)

James Sabben-Clare (1949-54) wrote down some reminiscences for the school magazine in 1983, in which he mentions overlapping with Colin McGarrigle (CSM) for five years as boys and then again when they returned as students to do a term's teaching.

Our paths were never closer perhaps than in that Easter Term (1954) when we were in partnership behind the scrum. We had a good XV, we reckoned, but someone had thoughtlessly caught mumps and most of the fixtures had to be cancelled. Aysgarth braved the journey and the germs and we took them apart, with CSM and me scoring most of the points. As for our student teaching days, I fear that my chief memories are of dances at the Crown Hotel and late-night parties on the sands. But we must have done some teaching too and enjoyed it, for here we are both in the same trade still.

The foundations of my own career were laid at Bramcote where I learned the virtues of thoroughness and accuracy in work. The methods were old-fashioned, as was the headmaster, Oswald Cooper; but we were taught with an intensity matched by few other schools in the country, and could no more forget our lessons than we could the man himself. His broken ruler, gripped in the two remaining fingers of a hand maimed at Gallipoli, his flamboyant handkerchiefs, his extraordinary arrangement of trousers and braces, his peculiarities of diction (resulting in part from ill-fitting dentures) – these were the stuff of indelible memories and unwearying imitation.

Boys joining Bramcote then did not have any gentle introduction to the institution of prep school life. There was a gulf between the junior and senior boys to the extent that often even a brother might be too embarrassed to be seen much with his younger sibling. Even so, having an older brother there helped, as Colin McGarrigle noted when interviewed:

I had watched my brother go to school term in and term out. He enjoyed it so I was going to enjoy it. I wanted to go. Some had the most appalling bouts of homesickness but in my case they were very short. They were usually dispelled because there was something to look forward to. One or two moments of great inspiration in the school would take your mind off most problems.

I remember sitting in the schoolroom on a Sunday night in a dressing gown quite warm because all the rooms had coal fires and huddled up together as one of the headmasters read something like *Prester John* or *The 39 Steps* or something – wonderful. He would have a little light on where he was reading but the rest of the room was in darkness. There must have been 50 or 60 of us in there – you could hear a pin drop. If you were miserable going into that session you certainly weren't miserable coming out – you were uplifted. Strangely some of the Sunday evensongs also dispelled any sort of gloom. Little things in those days meant a great deal more than they do today. One sweet was quite a major event, and a Negroid from Philip Beedle was also a treat.

The whole of one's life was a disciplined thing. As a youngster that framework of discipline created its own happiness in spite of dollops of unhappiness from time to time either because you had failed a test or something or your work wasn't very good or someone was giving you a hard time. One was very exposed to pressures from contemporaries – if you were being bullied you did have a pretty unpleasant time. Corporal punishment – it was the norm. We never questioned things.

But the fifth column was pretty effective – tapping skirting boards to tell others someone was coming. We had to stand up for ourselves even if not overtly – a sense of clan. Only when you become a master yourself do you realise how much children get away with right under your nose.

We had enormous respect for those who taught us. Most of them were very well read and extremely articulate. In the top form you never finished prep when prep was officially over. Oswald Cooper would give you ten history and five Scripture topics to research during the week. You always had an ongoing set of work. And we played a lot of football in the gym. That was almost a religion to a lot of us – soccer in the gym after prep.

For church and high occasions we had brown caps with 'BS' in gold and wore those extraordinary covert coats made exclusively by Rowntrees (in Scarborough). After church the school was taken on a formal walk before lunch. After lunch it was red caps and macs, red stockings and playground shoes and we were allowed to get them dirty. On the walks a certain sort of boy happily walked alongside the master. If there are 90 of you, only so many could do that. We (boys) chatted a lot to each other. We had great conversations around great flights of fancy. And many of those friendships have continued.

We used to play dot cricket and battleships. We had comics like the *Beano*, *Dandy* and *Boys Own* – sent by your own parents – and the *Eagle*. And we read a lot. One year I must have read every book that Henty wrote. I thought nothing of reading two to three books a week. We used to curl up in front of fires and try and salve our poor chapped knees. If you got your head into a good book no-one could get at you – you weren't breaking any rules.

The Match Books during the 1950s record the phasing out of the Fives Tournaments – but not before James Sabben-Clare had beaten Colin McGarrigle in the final of the Junior Tournament in 1953 to gain the prize of four shillings. In the 1950s the school still held its own boxing tournaments too 'which often resulted in stains of blood on the gym floor', said Colin McGarrigle.

82. The Fives Courts.

Father and Son

Canon Gervase Markham (1920-24) and Freddy Markham (1957-62)

Markham Snr   We had little gardens across the far side of the playing field. Each had a little bit of soil about ten feet square on which we never succeeded in growing anything except radishes and mustard and cress as far as I remember.

Freddy   We had gardens too but most of the time was spent organising the drainage rather than growing plants. So we had very sophisticated water channels, and ponds, and waterfalls, and sluices and weirs. We would pour a watering can full of water down at one end and make complicated routes for the water to run out at the other. We never actually got round to planting nasturtiums or mustard and cress. So we got no prizes there – just a sea of mud.

Markham Snr   One aspect I still value – when we reached nearer the top of the school – we had to learn paradigms and the Aorist Passive Paradigm of Luo was something you had to learn by heart. I did not learn it by the end of the afternoon and I was kept in and I had to go and lie on the floor of Mr Slater's study till I learnt it. I could hear the boys outside playing cricket and I wanted to go and join them. So I really set myself 'I am going to learn this' and I learnt it (and can still recite it). Then I could go out and play cricket. I was grateful for it afterwards.

Freddy   Were you grateful afterwards? We had to learn Latin such as prepositions taking the ablative or the accusative '*A, ab, absque, coram, de; Palam, cum* and *ex* and *e; Sine, tenus, pro,* and *prae . . .*' and I still don't know what the significance of any of these words is or what they meant or what they took but I might have known then.

Going to school in the 1950s and 1960s in the Bolshie period when there were revolutions and rebellions no-one would really admit that they loved going to school and they had every reason not to admit it because we lived in a very narrow, very harsh world where discipline was physical. There were a whole range of different forms of physical punishment regularly applied if there was any deviation from the routine. Nowadays they seem to run a very happy school.

Markham Snr   From what I just heard I don't think I disliked it quite as much as Freddy did. We knew he did at the time but we thought it was the best we could do for him in the long run.

Freddy   (with a wry chuckle) Unless you disliked it, it wasn't doing you any good. Anything you enjoyed was highly suspect.

Markham Snr   I don't remember being beaten quite so often. We knew that if we were doing something bad we would get beaten and I was beaten only I suppose three or four times in the course of my time there by the headmaster. We weren't beaten by other masters as far as I remember. And we took it as a natural thing — I don't remember anybody being unjustly beaten.

Freddy   I think one learnt a moral code which is admirable — the idea of owning up. There was a great stress on honesty, truthfulness, integrity, honour — what you might call old fashioned virtues. If they (the masters) said 'who's been talking after lights out?', and if you had been, you got out of bed and said so even if you knew you were going to get the gym shoe or the slipper for a reward. And the others weren't beaten. You would be in very great trouble if you had been talking and didn't admit it afterwards.

Markham Snr   It would be absolutely shaming — you couldn't live with your friends if you didn't behave like that.

Freddy   It was as much to do with a code of ethics among the boys themselves rather than being directly taught by the staff. But it definitely existed, this sort of code of honour, as it were.

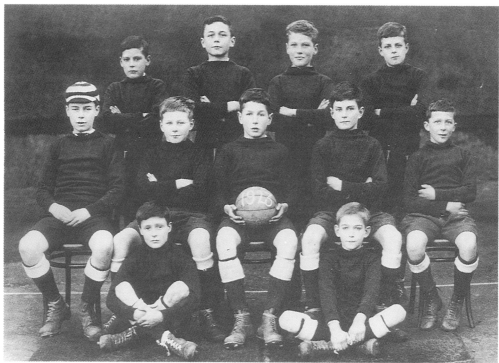

83. *The 1923 football team. Standing: Arthur Crosthwaite, William Wrigley, Arthur Nicholson, Joseph Gibson. Seated: William Thorburn, Gervase Markham, James Guise, Alexander Rendel, John Wright. On the ground: Duncan Carter-Campbell and John Knapp.*

84. *Three generations in 1993 – Standing: Gervase Markham, Freddy Markham, Stephen Hollins-Gibson and William Hollins-Gibson. Seated: Canon Gervase Markham and Joseph Gibson.*

Freddy Markham remembered crossing the Humber on the way to school on a paddle steamer with splendid shining brass engine rooms where slow and massive pistons turned and bells clanged. For Markham Snr it was a flat-bottomed steamer and the final stage of the journey was made in a real horse-cab clop-clopping along the Filey Road. One of the boys he teamed up with was Joseph Gibson. Joseph was there, along with his brother Henry, because his maternal uncle (R.R.Ware) was an Old Bramcotian. Henry A. Ware began the family tradition of attending Bramcote School back in 1902. He was followed by John Wilson Ware who was the first Bramcote boy to gain a scholarship to Winchester (in July 1911) when he came third on the Election Roll. By 1992 when Joseph Gibson's grandson William Hollins-Gibson joined the school 25 from this extended family (which included seven Wrights and four Robinsons) had studied there. Joseph Gibson lost contact with his friend, Gervase, for many years until their sons were at Bramcote – and with Arthur Markham (Freddy's second son) and William still there the links between the families have deepened. Of his own schooldays in the 1950s, Stephen Hollins-Gibson said:

I was extremely happy there. I loved it actually. I think I enjoyed being with lots of little friends. There were a lot of organised things, for when there were no games we went on walks in crocodile fashion, round the Mount, to the Mere and round the Spa. We didn't question it, it just happened. One master, Marshall, used to have an old convertible Morris 1000 which he kept in the corner of the playing fields. Once a week he used to go into the town with orders from us for small toys and models – they still do a very similar system now. We used to carve all sorts of things with balsa wood and build the most elaborate runs inside our desks for marbles and the aim was to see whose marble could stay on the move for the longest. It was unbelievable what ingenuity went into it. And the other thing we would do was to wire up our desk with batteries so that the light would come on when you opened it.

In what spare time we had, we didn't have a lot laid on for us. We had to provide our own entertainment. There was a common room and there was a snooker table. We used to play a game called slosh on it and it was quite popular. There was also a hobby room downstairs that no-one seemed to use! In the summer term we went to the South Cliff beach. We used to mess about catching crabs in pools when the tide went down. The swing on the top playground was great fun. It was a double one and it was very popular. It could carry four people because two could sit in the middle. We used to push that to its limits. Well, if I saw my children on that today I would be worried, I think. And then there was a roller skating craze on the top playground.

When we were in an upper dormitory we grew cress in the guttering. Outside the window there were about five or six slates below and you used to lean out and put the cress in the gutter and it grew marvellously. It was right over a sheer drop – it was a long way down, certainly. We grew it for the hell of it, I suppose. We used to grow all sorts of things in our gardens and we didn't know when to eat the stuff, but it seemed more fun to grow vegetables than flowers.

There was a lot of learning by heart – prayers and poetry – which I value now for I still know a lot of it and I certainly still read poetry. I think it was at Bramcote that I actually began to enjoy it. And I still have my history date card. I think this repetitive learning was very important as a discipline.

At the end of the day it was bliss to get to your bed and curl up – you were safe. Corporal punishment didn't bother me. In fact, I think we quite liked it because it was done and over with and forgotten. I don't think it hurt anyone – it made you sting a bit and the punishment was over.

In the past we weren't allowed to spend a single night out during term and it was pretty boring for our parents to come across for a weekend. They were holed up in some hotel in Scarborough and they didn't know what to do with us half the time.

I took my wife to the school when William was little just to show her and she thought it was absolutely super because the masters take such an interest. They pass boys in the corridor and they talk to them and smile and say hello. When I was there we used to huddle against the wall and let the masters past. The masters were certainly very devoted to the school but we feared them a little.

85. *Above: In the late 1950s the BBC Home Service recorded a 'Nature's Scrapbook' programme at Bramcote School. One of those on the panel, George Cansdale was known as the 'Zoo Man' and was especially popular with the boys. Christopher Butterworth (standing) took the chance to stroke the snake – as did Charles Dent (seated at the end of the row). Beside Charles Dent is Freddy Markham. Those behind them include Maurice Manners-Smith and William Waterhouse.*
86. *Right: Among those who had the opportunity to ask the panel a question was Stephen Ford.*

In June 1957 the south wing of the school was badly burnt with the head-master's hall and drawing room particularly devastated. Jim Hornby wrote later about the fire:

It was during the last term of Mr Cooper's headmastership (the night of June 1st). I was in charge of the boys at Bramcote. At the time part of the house was unoccupied as alterations were about to be undertaken to make it ready for my wife and myself to move in. I was occupying, as a temporary bedroom, the dormitory at the very top of the front stairs.

The alarm was raised by Nicholas Butler who was in the dormitory opposite my bedroom. He suffered from asthma and I suppose that the smoke warned him before it worried me! He came into my room and pulled me by the hair shouting 'Fire – and a real one too!' On looking down the stairs I could see that the blaze was in two places – the front hall and the drawing room. At the same time that we rang for the Fire Brigade the fire was spotted by a taxi driver and it was not long before the Fire Brigade arrived.

Remember in those days there was no connecting link between Bramcote and Nether-bank. Fortunately, it was a lovely summer's night and there was no great difficulty in ushering the boys across to Netherbank where Mr Marshall read the roll to check that all were present. My chief memories are:

John Gamble (Mr Gamble's son) getting angry with me because I would not let him try his hand as a firefighter. Nurse Smith venting her wrath on me for entering her room to wake her up! She said that it was not her duty night. The boys being taken off in ones and twos to the homes of neighbours for the rest of the night, and Mr Hamerton and myself leaving bundles of clothes on various doorsteps so that the boys would have something to wear when they first got up.

The boys were all sent home for ten days while we cleared up the mess. We used the gym as a dining room as a temporary measure (the main dining room had been flooded to a depth of a foot) and all the dormitories on the top floor at the Filey end of the building were out of action. We struggled through the rest of the term somehow: some boys slept at Willersley (with the Coopers), some in a house which we were lent (in Weaponness Park) and some, I think, in Mr Hamerton's house. The worst problem of all was the clothes. Being a Saturday night, the boys had two suits on their chairs and in a great many cases both were burned. I seem to remember living in a suit belonging to Mr Gamble for days afterwards! He is twice my size and I looked pretty odd in it!

The local newspaper reported that flames were shooting six feet out of the windows and the blaze could be seen two miles away. In the paper Jim Hornby was described as the hero of the night – and that he had spent it wearing a coat with a bright diamante clip lent to him by the matron. He had commented later that, unlike the well drilled boys, he could not find his dressing gown. Three fire engines and one turntable were at the fire and one boy remarked later – 'It was a dashed exciting night.'

87. Top right – The front hall after the fire.
88. Bottom right – Miss Kenworthy, the Assistant Matron, taking care of some of the boys: Stephen Ford, Peter Digby, Bob Urquhart, Paul Whittaker, John Gamble and James Carr.

Mrs Clare Hornby said:'The fire was the month before we got married.' She continued:

We had planned to live in a part damaged by the fire. So when we first got married we lived in what used to be Oswald Cooper's study which had been turned into a library and we slept in the matron's bedroom. They worked on our bedroom first and we got into our bedroom, I think, before the boys came back.

Four of our children were born at Scarborough. We ate downstairs with the boys for most of the time, highchairs and all. Relationships with the boys were excellent – they were absolutely free to come through to our part of the house whenever they wanted. They weren't scared of Jim (but were of some other masters). But children in those days were brought up to have a high respect for adults.

Jim – he didn't like corporal punishment. He stopped it at Clifton Preparatory School (when he was headmaster there). Jim used a slipper if anything. I was violently anti it but it was the norm when we first got there. It was difficult for Jim to do something entirely different to the others. I know he felt of corporal punishment that you should never do anything to someone else's child that you would not do to your own.

89. Jim Hornby with his son, David, at Bramcote around 1960.

Jim Hornby

Paul Hutchinson wrote this obituary in the magazine of Clifton College Prep School after Jim Hornby's death in 1984.

When Jim Hornby died at the age of 59 in February, the world of education lost a headmaster who was held in the highest esteem by the children he educated, by the colleagues with whom he worked, by the parents he guided so wisely and by his fellow headmasters. He was a man of great compassion and sympathy, who was as much at home with a Cabinet Minister as with an eight-year-old boy and who could get the best out of both of them.

Educated at Winchester and Trinity College, Oxford, Jim spent the war years in the Navy. He was shipwrecked in the Atlantic, he took part in the cross Channel invasion and he played football for the Navy at Hampden Park. Soon after leaving Oxford he was appointed headmaster of Bramcote and was quickly recognised as a man with a future.

Jim appeared completely at home with all men. Many a parent remembers how important Jim made them feel as he took them on a two hour tour of the school. Having met him they knew they could talk with him when problems arose. How many hours he must have spent trying to find help for parents who had suffered unexpected financial problems.

Three times he was elected Chairman of IAPS, and during those periods he was able to introduce many new schemes. Within twenty four hours of the tragic destruction of the primary school at Aberfan, Jim masterminded a trust fund which provided links between prep and primary schools. He did all he could to build independent and state schools closer together. When the secretaryship of the IAPS Office fell vacant in 1982 Jim was the natural person to take it over. It was indeed tragic that ill health so cruelly curtailed his days there.

Jim was a great family man and often paid tribute to Clare and his children for the strength which they gave him. Most of all perhaps he will be remembered for his concern for others and for his ability to put his deep felt Christian principles into practice. His rock-like faith in the importance of Christ-like living spilled over into his funeral service.

As the 1960s drew to an end the momentum of change increased as some of the Old Boys noted. James Rogers was there from 1966 to 1971 and wrote:

The school changed dramatically over these years. When I came in September 1966, Jim Hornby and Frank Hamerton presided. The timetable was dominated by Latin. Michael Coates started the change but the inspired choice of McGarrigle as headmaster transformed the school from old to new. Perhaps it was that I was getting older, but the school seemed to become a far friendlier place.

Bevan Gamble dominated my time at the school. Second Game football in his gum boots and mac with 'Idea good, execution poor' and loud castigation of anyone who turned their back on a tackle. I had two years on his second game and received hardly a word of praise yet he would remember me as a reasonable player. He always retained our affection. His English lessons gave a thorough grounding in English lit. and those with retentive memories will remember many quotations from 'Gambo' – his favourite was Polonius to Laertes 'To thine own self be true . . .' And he was. He gave many boys a good start. He also ran athletics and swimming.

Charles Moubray who returned to Bramcote in 1991 as a master, remembered Bevan Gamble too. He commented: 'I have a lot to thank Bevan Gamble for, more so as I have got older. He was a true traditionalist who commanded very great respect, certainly as far as I was concerned. With a map of the world and a stick he used to go repetitively around the world in the same order – mountain ranges, straits, seas, capitals. You knew them all.' It was something for which Charles Moubray was to be thankful for later when working in the shipping industry where he found that his knowledge of the world map, a vital part of his job, was considerably better than many of his contemporaries.

On looking back now on his own schooldays there were changes he enjoyed – such as going on what was probably the first school holiday when David and Mary Quine took a group to stay in a Scottish croft. But he was sad to see that some traditions were no more. He recalled:

Every Friday – 5th lesson, we used to have congregational practice (in the days when we went regularly to church). When we had practised everything we ought to have done we sang other songs, like *Road to Bangor, Darling Clementine, My Grandfather's Clock*. At the last congregational practice of term the leavers always stood on the stage together and each one chose a song for the whole school to sing together – a good singalong – we don't do that anymore.

At the end of term, we were taken on one or very occasionally two buses to Scarborough railway station. A master escorted us as far as York, from where we would continue our journeys either alone or in small groups; I often travelled alone for the whole journey from Peterborough when returning to school. On the journey to the station at the end of term, we would wait until the bus turned into Holbeck Road and as it began its descent down the hill, we started the singalong in the bus. At 6.45 in the morning most of the locals were probably awoken as we passed them, an entire busload in full voice. We sang, to the tune of *Road to Bangor*:

Riding down from Bramcote, On a Cronky Bus,
After weeks of waiting, They're getting rid of us,
Whizz Bang Pop! Down the Filey Road,
Closer now to freedom, With a heavy load.

This was always followed by *Ten Green Bottles* which, if timed correctly, ended as the bus drove into the station forecourt. The school booked a whole carriage (from Scarborough to York). As the leavers crossed the Ouse on the way they threw their caps into the river. I absolutely worshipped Bramcote. They were the happiest five years of my life. My mother picked me up from school on the last day and (at York) gave me the chance of chucking my cap in Ouse but I kept mine.

Letters from Charles Moubray to his parents in 1970:

20th September

Dear Mummy and Daddy,

There is a lot of news which I completely forgot to tell you about last Sunday. We are doing a wonderful anthem by Mendelssohn called 'I waited for the Lord' and I am enjoying it very much. Please could you send me a book of stamps otherwise I may be broke by the end of term as I have spent 12/- on stamping already. Also (if you can't afford to send it) could you please bring me my dictionary on my leave-out on Sunday.

I am now 'Captain' of the stamp club and Charles Lush is a member of the committee. I have already attempted to stop many bad shtamp shtamping [sic] habits such as unwrapping sweets, putting them in ones mouth and then looking at a stamp with sticky fingers. I am really quite senior now. I am on the High Table where masters and six senior boys sit; house vice captain (hard work) and in Form Remove.

The music master, Mr Lees-Jones is very nice indeed and he is very popular. His room is on the other side of our dorm and on the other side of the wall to my bed (in Netherbank) and he very often plays piano concertos by Beethoven at 10.00 to help get to sleep.

The film last night was *Carry on up the Khyber* – very funny to begin with but deteriorated towards the end although it was very much better than some of the other Carry Ons.

7th December

Dear Mummy and Daddy,

Tomorrow exams start with science followed by English and maths which I do not think I will do at all well in. The film last night was *Scott of the Antarctic* which I did not watch as half the time I was doing revision and the other half I was being filled up with peas and roast potatoes in the McGarrigle's house and watching the goggle-box (my usual hobby). I am afraid that I have hardly touched *Scharnhorst* or the *Ark Royal* (two modelling kits) this half of term because, after half term the boys who have passed CE . . . are doing a project ie a large cardboard temple etc. and there is so much mess in the hobbies room that no-one can move in there.

Tonight the choir are going to a village church called Reighton to sing carols. Our English master, Mr Croft, is vicar there. Then on Tuesday we go to an old (peoples') home called Combe Hay. Snow – 8 inches deep this morning. No more news.

Best love,
Charles.

By the time Charles Moubray returned to the school many of those old desks, so noted by Her Majesty's Inspectors, had also gone. For at an auction held in Scarborough in 1980 the items from Bramcote included a mid-19th century figured mahogany bow front chest, a late Victorian oak fall front writing desk, a Schoolmaster's late Victorian pine desk with hinged sloping and overhanging writing surface and . . .

> Lots 30-47 . . . an unusual opportunity to purchase the main requisites of a Victorian schoolroom. These desks patented in 1883 were supplied to the school in its early years circa 1895 and have been in use ever since.

90. John Fuller-Sessions and Colin McGarrigle preparing for the auction.

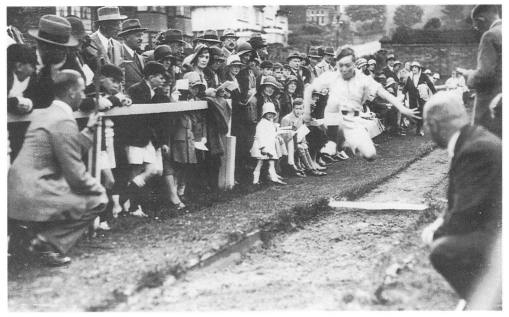

91. Alistair Thorburn in the long jump, 1930. In the 1930s Sports Day was still quite a ceremony and the ladies turned out immaculately dressed. That did not change for another two decades.

92. By 1964 the mothers were more relaxed about how they dressed.

CHAPTER 5

A Jazzier Tempo
1969–1983

'I came to Bramcote in the summer of 1966, and now, as I recall of my thoughts of the past, I cannot think of any notable thing that has not changed, except the work!' F.M. Willis in 1970.

William Willis conceived the idea in 1969 of starting a Bramcote newspaper and with two friends, William Worsley and Charles Lush, and the help of two masters (J.D. Saner and then Jeremy Valentine) produced the *Bramcote Chronicle*. Within a year this was succeeded by *The Bramcotian* which still flourishes. But Willis and Co. had set the pattern for chronicling the great burst of activity which the new young headmaster, Colin McGarrigle, brought in his wake.

In their magazine they reported that the railway club was flourishing, along with photography and natural history. The hobbies room was now thriving, and so was carpentry. Squash had been added to cricket, rugger and football. When boys put forward ideas now they could never be too sure what might happen. It was in 1970 that Hugo Hildyard suggested the seniors should try the 40 mile Lyke Wake Walk from Osmotherley to Ravenscar. He himself wasn't able to go on the first one nor, probably, did he then realise what a major tradition he had begun. In 1976 the Walk almost ceased to exist when fires on the moors made it too dangerous to go ahead, even though the walkers were ready, so John Tibbs and some other masters quickly surveyed a new route which they called the Bramcote Way. This was altered and shortened the following year and had the added asset of finishing at the school. By the 1980s the Bramcote Walk had become a rite of passage for leavers.

By 1977 *varia*, the newsbite section of the magazine, was fully established and into that the then editors (two masters: Robin Horspool and John Tibbs) sneaked in some earth shattering news – the era of the mini-leaves had begun, in addition to spending half-terms at home up until the late 1960s. The boys had been allowed to go out with their parents for about seven hours two to three Sundays a term. At half term they had seen their parents at the Fathers' Match on Friday as well as at the Sports on Saturday, and could spend an extra two hours with them on the Sunday.

An upbeat tempo began to pulse throughout the school – and not least in the music department. When a new music teacher was required, Colin McGarrigle, who liked to play jazz, knew what he was looking for: 'I was determined that music should be fun because I think good music in a school requires you to understand, play, and enjoy *all* forms of music. But too often in schools the choice of music can be very limited!'

102

93. Colin McGarrigle on the drums.

94. The first Lyke Wake Walkers in 1970: Tom Pollock, Nicky Walker, Simon Mackenzie-Smith, Robin Fisher, John Holtby, Richard Lytle, Tim Bulmer, Roderick Wright, Charles Terry, Rupert Blackett, James Rogers, Michael Banks, and Tom Murray.

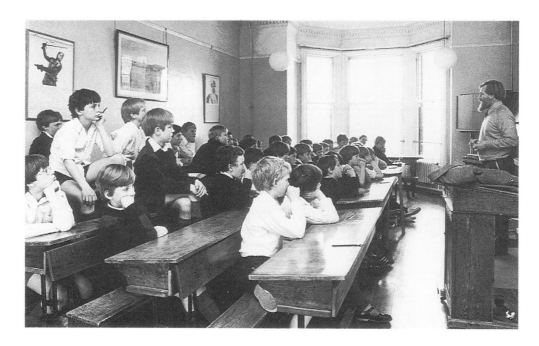

Thinking back on his time as a boy at Bramcote Colin McGarrigle explained that there wasn't just an undercurrent of fear that they lived with but also the pressure of never going home to their parents for 13 to 14 weeks each term. The fear needed to be removed and the mini-leaves helped by relieving the pressure. When interviewed he pointed out:

'The parents liked the change. That was the beginning of compromise towards the changing attitudes of modern parents. They wanted to see their child a lot more but they also wanted us to go on doing the job we were doing. At the beginning the parents were quietly expecting us to produce the goodies. Ten years later there was more overt expectation – that was the enormous change in the style of these schools. Parents now are more knowledgeable and they usually have done their research before committing themselves.'

John Gerrard, who joined the staff in 1973, pointed out that, with all the new activities going on in the school, there were even more demands on the masters and yet they never had a break. Philip Wood said:

'The restricted leave-outs meant that every Sunday you had a different lot of boys out so we never had a Sunday off at all. Some boys were here for every Sunday of the term. The mini-leaves were a much better idea. You could clear the whole school. It meant we could all get a break and you could plan ahead.'

Since he joined the school in 1974 he has seen what he believes were some fundamental changes, not least the demise of EMP – Early Morning Prep! 'In those days we had a rising bell at 7.15. We got the whole school up and we had to settle them down for about 20 minutes prep. Never written, it was always learning prep – spelling, French vocab. And then breakfast. About 1979 or 1980 we dropped EMP. That really was an old fashioned way of doing things – making them work before they had even eaten.' And another master commented: 'Why should we ask the boys to do something we wouldn't like to do ourselves.'

In the early 1970s there were no carpets, and no posters or pictures on the walls. 'The place used to look like a morgue with all the walls yellow ochre and all the paintwork dark brown,' commented Bernard 'Barney' Cooke, who first came as a groundsman at the school in the mid 1950s and then, after about ten years, moved inside to work until his retirement in 1985. The dowdy paintwork certainly changed in the McGarrigle era. In 1980 *The Bramcotian varia* noted that there was a feeling of a fresh start with redecorated passages and classrooms.

One major innovation in a prep school was the introduction of 'blinkers'. These were copied from similar fixtures in such Public Schools as Winchester (*toyes*). John Fuller-Sessions (who became assistant headmaster in 1972, two years after joining the school) explained:

'Blinkers allowed a boy to go somewhere away from the hurly burly and lose himself – write a letter or something.' It was a place where a boy could choose his own decorations and have his personal belongings. These days the blinkers are often festooned with the colours of various major football teams and towels advertising various breweries and distilleries. Several are equipped with 'ghetto blasters' that just fit in the top shelf.

95. *Top left: Boys don't have to hide away in the blinkers . . .*
96. *Bottom left: And there's still a place for desks. John Gerrard teaching in 1978.*

In the 1970s, the school was divided up into houses for the first time. 'By this stage we had quite a big school with 130 boys,' remarked Colin McGarrigle. 'Although we had school teams we could only get so many boys playing for the school. I felt it needed something within the school for more people to get a buzz out of playing in a match. And those four houses fell into place beautifully, with junior and senior teams.' The four houses are: Pidcock, Cooper, Hornby and Hamerton.

Bramcote, in the era of the baby boom and a healthy economy, was bursting at the seams with 140 boys in the school by the late 1970s. To Simon Redfern (1965-70) who returned to teach for one term in 1976 it seemed as if so much had changed and yet he noted:

'Fortunately, one thing which has not altered, despite the largish increase in numbers, is the family atmosphere in the school. In fact, there is now less of a "gap" between the juniors and seniors than there was six years ago. Everyone from the youngest to the oldest boy still seem to enjoy himself immensely and this is thanks to the tremendous efforts of the staff – something which I have found out this term and which I did not previously appreciate.'

But the attitudes of the boys were altering – no longer did they just accept things without question. Throughout the country there was an atmosphere of change. Colin McGarrigle pointed out that schoolboys at both Gordonstoun and Eton had 'mutinied' in various ways. 'It was a very strange time,' he observed. 'They were rather cynical and difficult times.' Corporal punishment was slowly phased out and the staff were to go through some periods of deep soul-searching as they adapted themselves to the changes. Gone too, by then were those cold baths in the morning (their decline began in Hornby's time) and the brown caps and covert coats for Sunday best. One of the first objectives in the 1970s was to make the school more flexible. Colin McGarrigle commented (echoing Hornby's thoughts):

'We couldn't go on just reproducing the two dimensional boy. Some boys are good at work, some boys are good at games. Some boys are good at both. An awful lot of boys are average at both. But if you only have those two theatres of operation, that's pretty limited.' Standards were not allowed to fall, however, and when Colin McGarrigle left in 1983 to take on the headmastership of Queen Margaret's Girls School at Escrick, south of York, Peter Terry (then a parent and school governor) wrote:

'Academically, during Colin's reign, Bramcote stood as high as ever and that is very high indeed. That is what inevitably matters to the bulk of us.' Every boy entering the Common Entrance Examination had passed and there was a steady stream of scholarships continuing Bramcote's links with Public Schools like Winchester, Sedbergh, Oundle, Harrow and Shrewsbury.

The system of boys going up as fast as they could with only those at the top of each class moving up to the next was gradually phased out during the 1950s. After that the brighter boys were never more than a year ahead of their contemporaries and they had to be socially as well as academically capable of moving ahead. The new system meant that staff spent many hours a week giving individual tutoring so that each boy could keep up with the subjects taught in class.

As James Sabben-Clare (now headmaster of Winchester) noted in 1983: 'The

Hobbies, Clubs and Societies

Remember who you are and where you came from... with a thumbs up... when our... her we sped off

STAMP CLUB

There can be no doubt that collecting stamps has become an increasingly popular and expensive hobby. Most boys at Bramcote content with collecting used stamps, and in developing ...anded down from father or grandfather.

The staff as usual monopolised (of Guy Fawkes night, all the fun (and hazards!) ...

...on Sunday evenings for an hour when there is no Evenson... get the chance to look at each others albums, and to so... ...atalogue their stamps. Mr. Potter spends most of his time ...ight, ...unger members how to find their way through 'Stanley Gi... for the others there is always a wide variety of books and c... ...us to use. By the time the bell goes most of us have at leas... further on, even if the process seems endless!

M.J. Ware.

RAILWAY CLUB

...ins is mainly a winter activity when there are ...ing out on the field. In the train room ...nd made extra trees and bushe... ...d, while both trains an ...wide selection ...possib

My particular masterpiece is a wine rack which sags a bit when you put the bottles in. It stands in the wine cellar which is in the attic at home. I made it to help my parents with their home-made wine, but since I did so they stopped making it.

Carpentry

net... have a go t...

M.S. Maclure.

Ruth Fuller-Sessions

BRAMCOTE WEATHER READINGS 198... .981

Autumn Term 1980

The warmest day   : Sept... ...
The coolest day
Th...

BRIDGE CLUB

Every Sunday during the winter, eight boys make their way to H.G.H-J's flat and spend the evening variously employed in playing bridge - the conversational variety - and refreshing themselves materially and spiritually. To be 'dummy' is sometimes an enviable position, affording an opportunity of sharing the adventures of Asterix and other educational characters. In spite of these distractions the basic rules were adequately mastered and more contracts were made than lost.

T.G. WOOD, R.T.B. PERCIVAL, A.E.D. CAMERON.

ART

In September we were very fortunate to receive from the Nobbs family four easels and a selection of books on various artists - Cezanne, Lowry, Rembrandt, Leonardo and Picasso. The easels have been a great incentive, for a number of the b... especially, to try their hand at oil painting, and the b... invaluable as sources of reference.

The following term saw Chris Cragg and Gordon Summe... placed first and second in the Scarborough Civic Societ... Competition. Both pieces of work contained some fine dr... have tried to encourage more observational drawing, for the key to all forms of artistic expression. One only h... through some of the above books to see this.

We attended and exhibited work at the 1980 a... bergh Festivals. The experience of seeing other schools' v... public school art department is both valuable and enjoya...

B.W.

CANOEING

We started out on this reckless expe... ...you... from Mr McGarrigle. When we turned the fi... down the river, but our enthusiasm was dan... muscles began to ache.

Mr Lytle kept reassuring us that the camp was not... away and that we would stop soon. When we ca...e round a long, laborious corner we saw an island. ... Cameron scouted about. When ...d there while a small suspension bridg... ...in we came to lumbering the canoes ...et out. After Mr Lytle's car ... ...frogs have spawned in ...arried them to which wa... ...ible success for the ...off to our burrow. Frog Scheme launched four - reston's house.

For the first time in five years ...s, we set about building a fire. I had the pond and this is a considerable ...t build a fire. We got the fire going eventually. Bramcote Save Our British Frog ...pset the spag (rather than the bog). We were very an-years ago (in 1974). ...u. After finding the wine in the car I tried to open it. After that, we ate our rescued spaghetti and bolognaise and then after a long talk by the fire, we went to our tents and sleeping bags.

Next morning we emerged very slowly and slowly the fog descended. After a chaotic breakfast, Rani, the Preston's dog, came and licked the plates clean. We eventually tried to set off (in the car) but Nicholas ...didn't start. So we pushed it out of the quarry with imme... ...led the "AA", but it started soon so we called ...

We s... ...the poacher on his side. Kirkham Abbey, ...long haul to were too hot to go any tu... ...we as it was. When we arrived at Ki... ...preferred to have and loaded them onto the two cars which... taking the canoe out I slipped, which was the only u... holiday. Eventually the first load went and Mr Lytle cam... alone. We decided to stay a while longer and go for a swim again. We finally left and soon arrived at school where we started the long, boring job of cleaning and unloading.

MARK PRESTON

Comment that the gamekeeper CSM, was heard to ... ...Jopling was Bramcote's first Deputy Head Boy, ...led the headmaster, ...e Canoeing Holiday

We all met up at ...'s. There were fi... ...ly. We had thr... ...g gas cooker ...pt in the fr...

FENCING 1981

...in the fencing coach took on a new lease of life and regular meet... ...re held each week. A squad of 30 members enrolled f... ...ntary activity. Numerous Club pools were fough... ...ent to fight against Scalby School.

The summ... ...xture in Filey and my thanks to Miss Allwood fo... ...a team to the match. Farnell came away undefeat... ...promising prospect. Bromage is probably the b... ...school and Flinton the most unorthodox. In ou... ...petitions Worsley ma has achieved the most wins ... ...ng have fenced during this year.

Armin Kille, a real Chef, arrived and the Bramcote taste buds were soon enthusiasti-cally titillated.

...most conscientious and helpful fencing secretary. Harvard, ma. Bromage, Cumberlege, Garnett mus. orsley ma, Stevens, Jones mi, Flinton, Wordie, Farnell, Pettifer ma. Harvard, ma. McMahon-Turner, Jackson, Pumfrey ma. Hall, Garnett mi, Cobb, Wright, Wood mi, Leggard. Marshall, Pickard, Cresswell, Dewar ma, Worsley mi, Fraser Bentley, Baker-Cresswell, Read, Fletcher mi, Crumby.

J.F.F.S.

SKIING

The school organised another ...this year and again a lot of fun u... ...time we seem to be becom... ...village and the locals ar...

...liday in Andermatt ...this was our third ...ry scene in the ...oming.

MODEL CLUB

This term's addition to the Bramcote facilities is a cosy upstairs room, now given over to modelling, with a bathroom next door which makes it easy to wash out brushes, and go to the loo. A radiator, powerful lights, and plenty of room, help create a suitable atmosphere for modelling, with perhaps a quiet chat with a friend while you work.

97. *Cuttings (mainly) from the* Bramcotian.

98. *David Lees-Jones with the string band in 1971.*

narrowness of our early education (at Bramcote) has given place to a wonderful richness of opportunity and experience, and great is the debt that boys and parents owe to Colin McGarrigle for his initiative. But the old values have not been forgotten, and a solid academic grounding is as important a part of Bramcote's training as it ever was.'

When David Lees-Jones joined the staff in the Christmas Term of 1970 only piano lessons were provided. After just one year he had built up a lively string band. Within four years two boys, Dominic Robinson and Thomas Keith, could write:

'Bramcote music has been building to a peak with an ever increasing number of boys being involved over a broad area; for example each week there are: 77 individual lessons given, two choir practices of one hour each, two band practices of 25 minutes each and one orchestral practice lasting one hour. To help cut down the waiting list of boys wishing to take up the instrument of their choice, Mrs Forrester comes in one or two afternoons each week as do the other four members of the peripatetic music staff, to give piano lessons to the more junior pianists.'

Instruments played included the clarinet, oboe, trumpet, trombone, viola and cello. There was also the organ. This had been donated to the school in memory of Frank Hamerton. David Lees-Jones also built up the choir during his four years at Bramcote, and started a new tradition – that of participating in the

99. The Madrigal singers at the Merchant Venturers Hall, York, 1983.

annual Royal School of Church Music (RSCM) Festival at Ripon. They still had time however to sing carols at old peoples' homes in Scarborough and to present anthems at St Martin's regularly.

The boys increasingly shared in a wide range of musical activities, including going to concerts to listen to the Black Dyke Mills Band, the Hallé Orchestra and the *Messiah*.

Philip Wood, when he took over from David Lees-Jones in 1974, continued to develop music as an important part of the life of the school. Some of the best musicians in the school began to be selected to play with the IAPS Orchestra and Band and a few gained music scholarships to various Public Schools. Philip Wood said:

'We are not in any sense a music school, like a cathedral school or a choir school. Our boys are competing against highly skilled and highly trained musicians from specialist schools. For us such scholarships are major achievements. With so much going on in the school you have to fight for your corner . . . but it is all fairly good natured.' In 1982, David Pearson who, along with Henry Stevens that year, was selected to play in the IAPS orchestra for the second year running, noted: 'It is difficult to imagine what Bramcote would be like without the musical activities.'

David Pearson that year not only achieved his Grade VIII while at Bramcote (the first to do so was Martin Appleyard in 1980) and played 1st trumpet in the IAPS Orchestra but also was awarded the 1st Music Scholarship at Harrow.

100. Matthew Hall playing the Euphonium around 1982. His audience included Peter Dalgleish, Justin Murray, Charles Breese, Robert Peacock and Richard Worsley.

101. *Philip Wood teaching a music class in 1977. Those singing along with him included Diana Gerrard and Ruth Fuller-Sessions.*

The 1970s marked a remarkable event in the history of Bramcote – the daughters of John Fuller-Sessions and John Gerrard were enrolled. Diana Gerrard and Ruth Fuller-Sessions joined the school in 1975 followed by Sara Fuller-Sessions in 1977. 'I think it took everybody a while to get used to it, particularly the boys,' Diana Gerrard said. 'It was like "we've never had girls before – why have we got them now?" But I never noticed that from the staff, just some of the boys.'

The inability to provide dormitories for girls has made it impossible as yet for Bramcote to consider becoming a mixed school. So Diana, Ruth and Sara are still the only girls to have studied there.

Maurice Platnauer, Bramcote's first scholarship boy, died in December 1974. While he was a master at Winchester, 1910-22, he and a fellow-master, Murray Hicks, bought Twyford Down and Hockley Golf Course for conservation purposes. In 1955 they donated this land to Winchester School. Twyford Down is now the subject of a compulsory government purchase order for the controversial M3 bypass.

Platnauer was a Fellow of Brasenose College, Oxford, from 1922, becoming its vice-president in 1936 and principal from 1954 until 1960. He was the author of several distinguished books on the classics.

102. Gifts from parents made it possible to provide the choir with cassocks in 1979.

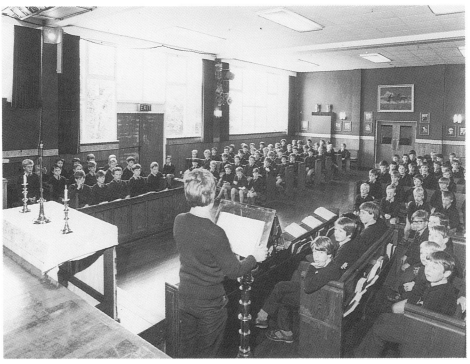

103. And brass candlesticks for the Hall.

By the autumn of 1971 the masters no longer needed a tot of rum to warm up after a swimming lesson. With the opening of the school pool the boys only swam at South Bay on warm days in the summer – until it was closed a few years ago. At a time when few new boys could swim the new pool provided ample opportunities not only for fun but also for swimming lessons to suit all. The Pool Prefects, for instance, were trained to such a high standard by the summer of 1972 that they were capable of running a swimming period by themselves, although there was always a master in charge.

There were problems with the pool the next year but it was still possible to continue the annual swimming sports. With the pool in constant daily use, by 1975 the school had achieved another landmark – in that every person in the school had passed his initial test and could swim four lengths. There was an attempt to start water polo but there was some confusion about the rules. In the end they made up their own so that even the youngest swimmers could join in without getting hurt. Tim Potter, a master, noted: 'The pool is one of the few areas where most juniors can share their enjoyment with the seniors without there being any great difference in ability.'

As the years marched on more and more boys attained bronze, silver and gold ASA Survival Scheme awards and in 1980 the senior boys began to notch up Life Saving badges as well. In the 1980s the emphasis was to change from life saving to 'education for survival'. *The Bramcotian* also records their first swimming matches – beating the area champions, Lisvane, in a return match in 1980.

The gardens continued to provide a lot of enjoyment to many boys as the decades passed.

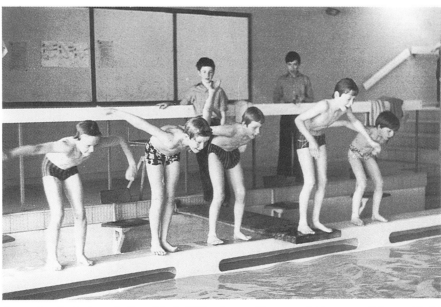

104. *Jason Lord, Andrew Beilby, Mark Hills, James Sharp, and Cameron diving; with Malcolm Maclure and Justin Appleyard watching (1978).*

My Garden

My garden is about six foot square;
It's fifth along the row.
At break times I often go out there
To plough and reap and sow.

My garden rests beside the way;
It sees the people walking by
And watches what goes on all day;
It sees the sun blaze summer's sky.

My garden is comparatively small,
But still it brings great pleasure;
In fact – it's hardly seen at all -
But the joy it always brings to me
Is impossible to measure.

William Rolston (then 12)
Bramcotian 1976

105. Frew and Smith gardening around 1928.

106. Gardening in 1934.

107. Pettifer and Co. gardening in 1978.

Before 1972 most unofficial sports took place in the gym with wild games of football or endless rugby scrums. The laying of tarmac on the playground and the addition of lights in 1978, gave an excellent opportunity for developing games for fun and both football and hockey leagues were established. These especially gave non-games players a chance to shine and provided the important social function of mixing the age groups. The five-a-side football games usually lasted 15 minutes which was enough to exhaust even the fittest.

108. *The playground in use after being tarmaced.*

109. *Snooker has become a constant favourite.*

An Overview 1935-1993

John Cundall attended the school himself between 1935 and 1941 and four of his sons were at Bramcote during the 1960s and 1970s. He joined the Board of Governors in 1968 and was the Chairman of Governors from 1981 to 1988.

I was one of the first parents with boys in the school on the Board. Up to that time the idea was frowned upon. Under the Cooper/Pidcock regime parents had little influence in the school. They accepted how the school was run and had little opportunity to voice their feelings. The constitution of the Board of Governors has broadened tremendously in recent years and we now have women on the Board.

When I was at school we accepted the fact that we did not see our parents much during the term, although I don't say that we enjoyed the situation. Life was harder then, but equally parents were stricter with their children. I do not think that you minded it being hard as long as it was fair.

Some masters did have favourites and obviously life was easier for boys that played games or were good academically than for others. On occasions there was some bullying, but if masters came to know of it, it was rapidly stamped out. My parents went to Mr Pidcock on one occasion to complain about bullying, and he dealt with this very firmly. In those days it was not easy to communicate with the masters, but equally I think you did not have the same relationship with your parents as children do now.

Parents now take much more interest in what is going on in the school. Everything has been done now to encourage parents to come and see their children and to take greater interest in what is going on.

Both Cooper and Pidcock were headmasters of the 'Old School' and it seemed that little change took place during their regime. Hamerton clung very much to the traditions of the Cooper/Pidcock period, but gradually changes took place. The school was very fortunate in having an excellent Chairman of the Governors in E.E. Sabben-Clare who was a great help in guiding the school through this period of change.

The school has a high reputation for education and sport, but it was considered by some parents that it had too narrow an outlook. It was gradually accepted that boys needed a much broader education and although the high standards have been maintained it has become possible for boys who excel neither as scholars nor at games to have a good and much broader education. This has been made possible by the devotion and dedication of the staff.

When I came to the school there were no clubs, with the exception, I think, of the Stamp Club. Now there are so many opportunities and interests that it seems difficult to fit these in with work and games.

Colin McGarrigle did as much to broaden the outlook of the school as anybody and he was a great ideas man. During his period as headmaster everything gained tremendous momentum and at times it seemed that there was almost too much going on in the school. The most important thing was that the average boy could find opportunities to develop his talents and to flourish and that the atmosphere in the school was happy.

CHAPTER 6

Just for the Fun of It...
1970–1993

Soon after he joined the school in 1970 John Fuller-Sessions began his annual outings to the Norfolk Broads where he and the boys could sail, live together and share the cooking! 'It was just for fun' he said. One theme which flows right through from the 1970s till today is the sense of adventure and experimentation that the boys and staff share which spills over into the holidays. Colin McGarrigle pointed to the key role of one of the masters, Richard Lytle, in developing many new activities.

110. Top left: Sailing on the Broads.
111. Bottom left: Richard Baldwin and Michael Hewitt at Filey in 1986, learning how to take total control of a sailing boat. The boys were taught the basics of rigging on dry land before attempting to sail.
112. Below: John Fuller-Sessions with Nick Cridlan (1987-91) on the Broads.

113. Richard Lytle helping Guy Speir with a canoe on the Derwent in 1987.

Up until 1970 Bramcote sports activities were mainly confined to the three main sports, with some tennis in the summer – and swimming in the South Bay Pool.

'The canoeing started in the late 1970s when we borrowed a mould from Strand Glass in Leeds and began to manufacture our fleet,' recounted Richard Lytle. 'The process was messy and smelly but Simon Gordon and Charles Nobbs stood it longer than most. The first canoeing holiday was on the Leeds-Liverpool Canal when the rain was unrelenting except for the last day. The following year saw the fleet added to by Richard Hollingbery and Jason Lord and the first Wye Trip. Since then the top forty boys have a weekend on the Derwent each summer, and there are extended trips during the holidays, a four-day trip on the Derwent and a six-day one on the Wye from Hay to How Caple. Three of the original canoes survive, though we had to replace six which failed to escape the clutches of a flash flood on the Wye in 1988.'

In 1985 orienteering, always an occasional activity, developed a more regular pattern and is now offered to the top 36 boys who, in groups of three, get to tackle four routes in a season. Archery, organised by Graham Brignall, began in 1988 with regular arrows either on the field in summer or in the gym during the Christmas and Easter terms.

A section of the air raid shelter had been adapted to incorporate a .22 rifle range and various competitions take place there throughout the year, usually fitted into break times or on days of bad weather.

114. Justin Murray taking on the Monington Falls during a Wye Trip.

Cricket, football and rugby still take pride of place in the school calender with several pages of *The Bramcotian* given to recording the exploits of the various teams. Of the football season in 1981 it was reported:

'A quick glance at the results will show that this has been near to being a vintage year throughout the school. Of the 38 matches played at various levels, the school lost six and in the process scored more goals than can be remembered.' 1989 also proved to be a memorable year, according to Richard Lytle:

'This was one of the better sides we have had in recent years and though Raincliffe proved too strong for us – twice – all the other matches (nine) were wins. Undoubtedly the best win was against the old adversary, Aysgarth, when, for a twenty-five minute period in the second half, the team played as well as any Bramcote side I have ever witnessed. But before we could savour the win, fate was to cloud the moment in that Robin Sutermeister broke his wrist in the last few minutes.'

The school continued playing football in the Michaelmas Term and rugby in the Easter Term and it was often noted that they did not do so well against those schools who played rugby throughout the winter season. Even so, in 1980 the 1st XV won ten out of their 14 matches. Bramcote often fielded a strong 2nd XV and in 1990 this team won all of its seven matches much to John Horton's delight:

'This was a most enjoyable season. The team played with a lot of enthusiasm and plenty of skill and of course everything was made that much more satisfying by going through the term without losing a match.'

Yet even these regular sports saw changes as it became possible for the younger boys to participate in tournaments and matches against other schools. There are now often Under-11 and Under-9 matches along with the five-a-side football tournaments and nine-a-side cricket league. The Under-11 cricket team have twice won the Scarborough Primary School Knockout competition for three years in a row (1977-79 and 1983-85). In the 1983 final Nick Fuller-Sessions hit a winning streak and carried his bat for an unbeaten 57 in a total of 94 for 2.

The squash option became increasingly popular in the 1980s under the guidance of first George Shelton and then, on his retirement, Andrew Hutton. Sunday Leagues were established in 1984 and this gave the better players greater opportunity to improve. The highlight came in 1988 when the school 'Five' (Will Collinson, Simon Henson, James Brown, Ben Ward and Alex Booth, and with Guy Hewetson) won its way through to the finals of the Bath Cup, a national competition for under-14s. Over half the school now play squash, with some boys playing in the local squash leagues. For the last two years, the Scarborough Under-16 champions have been boys who learned their squash at Bramcote – Edward Henson and Guy Beaumont.

The school's approach to athletics became more serious in the 1980s with the arrival of first John Horton and then Peter Wilkinson with formal training sessions gleaned from the cricketing timetable; a revision, updating and more organised approach to the 'Standards'; and an extra athletics evening offered on Fridays for those that wanted it.

115. *Nick Fuller-Sessions increasing his score with style during the 1983 finals of the Scarborough Primary School Knockout competition.*

116. *Richard Williamson clears the ball during a 1st XV match against St Martin's in February 1993. Julian Summerfield is fly half, with Jimbo Meysey-Thompson the 1st Centre.*

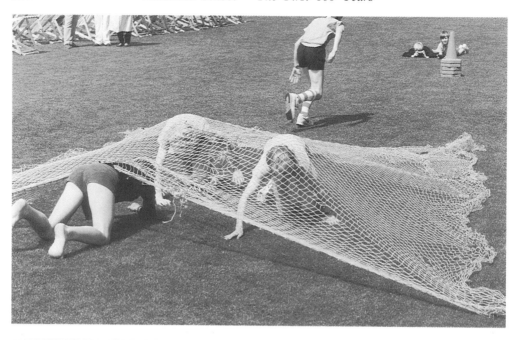

The old favourites like the Fathers' Match and the School Sports at Summer Half Term continued with the three-legged race and obstacle race still providing lots of fun. But none could match nature's own spectacular display in 1987 when, during a great thunderstorm, John Gerrard's beard stood on end as a result of one particularly violent flash of lightning.

117. The obstacle race c. 1990.
118. But negotiating the barrels, William Sutton-style, has changed.

119. *Jono Standeven and William Harding-Newman race for the finishing line in the three-legged race.*

120. *Over the hurdles – Simon Pilcher, James Reeve and Justin Gregory.*

121. Sports Day has always been an important event for the mothers – whether they came in all their finery as this one did around the turn of the century . . .

122. Or to take the opportunity to slip some sweets into their son's pocket as Mrs Dick was probably doing as she sat close to Marcus in June 1933.

In July 1991 a new half-day holiday was inaugurated – for Mothers' Day!
123. Above: Those at the 1992 Mother's Day included Penny Clark, Margaret Alton, Kate Dewhirst and Pat Greensit.
124. Left: Erica Hardaker in the Mothers v. Boys match, 1992.

Gardening has retained its appeal and for almost a decade now the judge for the best-kept garden competition has been Mr Ron Womack from a local gardening centre. He could always spot when a garden had been weeded well regularly – or if it had been quickly tidied up before his arrival.

Other clubs have developed over the past two decades to the point where teams from Bramcote now take part in inter-school tournaments. Hugh Howell-Jones inspired boys to play Bridge during the 1970s and a group regularly met in his house. Mary Gerrard now teaches the finer points of this card game and a team quite regularly takes part in the Yorkshire Schools Cup. Chess has also developed – with even the Toads wanting to learn – and in the 1992 *Bramcotian* John Horton wrote:

'Undoubtedly the highlight of this year was that both the Senior and Junior teams reached the finals of the Northern Prep Schools' Chess Cup. The Junior team actually won their final against Terrington and finished the season with the excellent record of only having lost a single 'board' in all matches. The Seniors had had a much tougher path to the final than the Juniors and their opponents in the final were the much feared Birkdale team. They put up a worthy performance against some good players but would have to admit that the Birkdale players were really in a different class. William Reeve played well on Board two to win his game and the captain, Richard Hall, preserved his record of never losing to another prep school boy (after five years in Bramcote chess teams) by drawing his match.' Birkdale won by four and a half games to one and a half.

Bramcote has been taking part in the general knowledge competition organised by SATIPS (Society for Assistants Teaching in Preparatory Schools) for many decades. It involves answering a written paper of 100 questions in 45 minutes. In 1992 this attracted entrants from 200 schools nationwide and the Bramcote junior team came 35th. The school's own General Knowledge competition in 1992 was research based. Over the Christmas holidays the boys had to search out the answers to a number of questions and sit a multiple-choice test on their return. The House General Knowledge Competition, run along similar lines to University Challenge, continued, as did the Family Christmas Quiz which more recently has joined the ranks of Bramcote favourites.

The Discussion Group that flourished in the 1970s seemed at last to have been reborn as the Debating Society in 1992. This latter society came into existence mainly as a result of the enthusiasm of some of the senior boys, like Richard Bennett. They held three lively debates during the year on banning smoking in public places; the banning of blood sports and the advantages/disadvantages of single sex education. In 1975 issues discussed included the role of the Monarchy; Nixon and Watergate; the sugar crisis and other world problems; and racial discrimination.

125 a & b. The egg and spoon race about 1900.
126. Diane Hanline certainly found it much easier to run than those 90 years earlier.

Some clubs were constantly revived – like model railways and stamp collecting. Others, like teddy making and cookery, were created by the wives as part of the fun. Mary Quine began the cookery club in September 1969, and it was continued in the 1970s by Marion Fuller-Sessions. These days cookery classes often form part of the Leavers' Programme.

Carpentry has been around, in one form or another, since Savery's days. Then it was wood-carving and by 1919 'carpentering' was an extra costing two guineas a term. In the 1980s the carpentry section needed more space. With the completion of the Music and Arts Centre it was decided that the Appeal Fund set up for that should remain open and this enabled the school to buy a Portacabin so that the carpentry section could have their own room. New minibuses were also bought through this Fund. Parents and Old Boys continued to support the Appeal – and were able to participate in the fun side of the school themselves.

Back in the early 1970s the Old Bramcotian Society was formed and the first Old Boys' dinner was held in 1981. In the mid-1970s dances were held for the Old Boys but this annual event migrated to the Summer Mid Term and parents joined in as well. For the fun of it, however, few boys could match the Old Bramcotians who, at one of their get-togethers, managed to throw both Colin McGarrigle and John Fuller-Sessions into the swimming pool.

127. *Top left: Russell Wilcock on the railway, 1986.*
128. *Bottom left: Marion Fuller-Sessions taking a cookery session.*
129. *The portacabin arrives!*

130. *The Sports Day photographers c. 1905.*

Bramcote has obviously owed a lot to its photographers over the years. These days it is Paul Norris who provides the photographic record. It is not known who donated to the school the old albums with those extraordinary photographs of the 1900 to 1909 period, nor exactly who took the pictures in the school albums from 1910 until the 1920s although it is obvious that Slater and Pidcock wrote many of the captions. Oswald Cooper left behind a packet of photographs of one Cayton Bay picnic. Some of the most artistic photographs, including that of Eshton Hall, were taken by Urling-Smith who taught at the school from 1927 until 1946.

'I learnt about cameras from Urling-Smith,' said Val Wrigley. 'First there was a very bulky reflex job and then to our delight the first of the 35 mm. Leicas.'

Photography was obviously not a major activity from 1946 until the 1970s but was then revived by John Fuller-Sessions, with J. Montague-Jones organising the photography club. This club has had a varied appeal since, but recently Roy Rigley has helped to reactivate it.

131. *Urling-Smith with David Hanson in 1929.*

132. The 1986 leavers try their hand at video filming.

133. While some continue to need a tripod.

Making videos has joined the list of new school activities, while some forms of entertainment have continued throughout the decades. Lectures about expeditions to wild, faraway parts of the world have enthralled schoolboys since Bagshawe watched lantern slides about 1912. One talk in 1991 however had an unexpected outcome. The speaker from the NSPCC had ended with the suggestion that the boys should do some sort of sponsored event.

It just so happened that it snowed . . . So what better than a sponsored snowman-building day! Their grand total came to £1,142. Bramcote boys, in fact, have often been involved in raising money for charities. They gave over £1,000 to the Queen's Silver Jubilee Appeal and regularly make a collection for the Church of England's Children Fund.

134. A successful snowman day.

The school play was never quite the same again after Hugh Howell-Jones appeared on the scene. John Fuller-Sessions noted in 1987 when H-J retired:

'He masterminded the most marvellous productions on stage. Every Easter Term he managed to find a play requiring at least 70 actors, some of whom needed to be able to dance and/or sing, numerous changes of costumes and even a variety of incredible props. Rehearsals were all quietly arranged, with no disruption to school life at all. All the wonderful props, from unseaworthy boats named 'The Puke' to dragons with flashing eyes, or exploding television sets, were designed and largely made by Hugh himself. Perhaps his humour and attitude to life was best seen in the innumerable scripts he produced for form plays, unfortunately only ever seen by the school.'

The form plays were usually produced at the end of the Christmas Term with the school bubbling with excitement. The *Bramcotian* of 1980 noted that the plays were varied, full of laughter and ominous silences, successes and semi-failures. Yet the enthusiasm and obvious enjoyment of the performers helped them overcome all obstacles.

And then there were all the theatre outings. Not just the *Black and White Ministrels* and the *Val Doonican Show* but, as in 1988, a cultural media tour of the North – from *Henceforward* and *Educating Rita* at Ayckbourn's Theatre in the Round to *A Comedy of Errors* by the RSC touring company, and the film *Brighton Rock*.

This has now grown into an established feature of the school with play reading sessions on Sunday nights followed by trips to see what has been read. In the Christmas Term 1992, the top forms went to ten productions which included two Royal Shakespeare Company tours, the National Theatre touring production of *An Inspector Calls* and visits to Harrogate, York, Oldham and Richmond theatres.

It was Hugh Howell-Jones who started the Latin Plays which have become part of the traditional Summer Half Term weekend along with the Fathers' Match and Sports Day. He and the Latinists wrote witty plays to be enacted with maybe more zest than classic erudition. These days the Latin plays are written by Paul Norris and produced by John Horton and are as zany as ever, mixing modern characters with historical events – such as Margaret Thatcher helping to fight off the Roman invaders!

The Latin/French play of June 1988 was entitled 'Asterix va à Scarborough – an entirely new concept in multi-cultural entertainment':

Scene One:

A messenger suddenly arrives at the garrison of the Roman forces in Eboracum, and announces that Caesar is coming to see why they haven't managed to capture Scarborough. The legions who have tried have been decimated by the wild tribe of Modernums who rule the coastal area. Eventually they decide that the wrath of Caesar would be worse than that of the Mods and set off.

Scene Two:

Out in faraway Gaul Asterix's tribe have grown a little restless. The Romans are not as much fun as they used to be and the weather in Gaul has been particularly bad recently. Asterix goes along to Congéfix the local travel agent who suggests that they try Scarborough, famous for its sun and unusually temperate weather – there is also a good chance of a fight with the Modernums. This latter fact is just what the doctor ordered and they book a weekend special.

Scene Three:

The Modernums are planning their rally. There is quite a lot of bickering about whose chariot is the best looking when suddenly one of their spies comes in with the news that Romans have been sighted heading in their direction. A few moments later another spy rushes in and tells them about the strange band of foreigners heading in their direction. They assume it is a French branch of the Modernums, and decide to enlist their help to repel the Romans.

Asterix and his gang have some difficulty understanding the strange British gang's language but fortunately one of them has brought along a holiday phrase book which they use to communicate with the Modernums. They discover they have one thing in common – a psychopathic hatred for the invaders. They plan to overcome the Romans by subtlety and guile.

Scene Four:

The Romans arrive and fall hook line and sinker for the plan and are overwhelmed. This all goes to explain why Scarborough was never part of the Roman Empire.

135. Chariot charge Mods style.

136. *Skiing in 1992 – Arthur Markham, James Dent, Quintin Fraser and William Evans.*
137. *Below: Sam Graham skiing in 1992.*

Nor has the school confined its fun to Britain. In 1970 Richard Lytle took three boys, Roderick Wright, Richard Umbers and Hugo Hildyard, to the Passion Play in Oberammergau. From this excursion the continental holidays of 1971 and 1972 developed. Two VW camper vans, driven by David Lees-Jones and Richard Lytle, toured Europe for three weeks, giving twelve boys each time a taste for the road. These trips then lapsed for several years until resurrected in 1987 by Paul Norris with a ten-day *gite* holiday near Lisieux. Since then the school has used a *gite* (a long barn) in the grounds of a chateau just outside the town of Loches which, it is hoped, will become the base for slightly more formal class visits in the Christmas terms.

Richard Lytle also instituted the skiing holidays, first to Maurach in 1971, but then to a variety of places including Aprica, Sause D'Oulx, Andermatt and Alpbach. With a few breaks, this has been an annual affair, the destination for the past few years being Les Crosets in Switzerland. In 1990 the skiing group made a special presentation to Delia Feather (the school secretary) and Richard Lytle for doing so much personally to make the trip so economical and enjoyable.

138. The door was opened wider in 1992 for local boys to participate in the fun, the sports, and the academic excellence of the school when day boys were able to attend for the first time. The first day boys were Jonathan Clark, Timothy Brignall and James Grunwell.

139. *Thomas Dugdale opening the door of the new Music and Arts Centre, followed by John Fuller-Sessions.*

CHAPTER 7

Opening the Door to the Future
1983–1993

Freddy Markham had so disliked Bramcote when he was there in the 1950s that he would not even visit Scarborough. Then he received the appeal from John Fuller-Sessions (who had just taken over as headmaster from Colin McGarrigle) for funds to build the Music and Arts Centre. He was so fascinated by this seeming innovation from the much narrower curriculum he had known that he just had to go and see. On meeting John Fuller-Sessions he decided that Bramcote was now the school for his two sons, Gervase and Arthur.

'It was then that I realised Bramcote was a forward looking school. The true mark of a good school is if they can do a good job with the exceptional or unusual boy. Any school can do something with the perfect boy.' When asked to explain further why he sent his sons there he replied:

'I believe it now has all round excellence – the striving for the highest standards in every field – and a very high quality of staff. It is the concentrated experience they can get at a boarding school which is not diluted every night by coming home and thinking about something else and being with different people. The intensity of the experiences and the amount that you can absorb in the time that you are there is very much greater at a boarding school. And because it is a good boarding school and because the staff have very detailed knowledge of each child and care about them individually, the very best is brought out of each child at a very crucial phase of their lives.

'The first impression that you get when you go to the school now is that the boys enjoy being there and this was rather shocking to me when I first revisited the school because the thought of boys actually enjoying their school days was a novel idea. As far as I know none of the offensive weapons are considered necessary or seen to be necessary, and discipline is somehow maintained without any of this.'

When John Fuller-Sessions and his wife retired from the school in 1990 one of the masters, Richard Lytle, wrote in *The Bramcotian*: 'Bramcote has always been a friendly place but both John and Marion actively encouraged an atmosphere in which boys took responsibility for themselves and others. It was not so much that seniors were put "in charge" of the younger boys but that they were asked to be more mindful, more sensitive to the needs of others, so that niggles or difficulties could be aired and discussed before they could become problems.'

Charles Moubray who had been at the school in the late 1960s noted how much closer the senior and junior boys were now. He returned as a master in 1991 and commented: 'One thing that struck me – the boys are longing to come. I was carrying in the trunks and there wasn't a single tear.' The process had taken several decades but for the majority of the boys at Bramcote the pain and fear that Freddy Markham and Colin McGarrigle had reflected upon was no longer there. The family within the school had changed as much as the families who sent their boys.

As with the McGarrigles and the Hornbys a major objective of the Fuller-Sessions and the Gerrards (John Gerrard became assistant headmaster in 1984) was to make it possible for every child in the school to be good at something. The Music and Arts Centre marked a major step in this process.

The new centre proved quite an inspiration for the music department. In 1986 they organised a recital given by the East Riding Baroque; in 1987 they acquired a very fine Bluthner grand piano; and they capped it all in the summer term of 1989 by having the Aeolian Wind Quintet give a short concert. As Philip Wood, pointed out, this was most unusual at a school for such an age group and spoke a lot for the maturity of the boys who enjoyed it. Over 70 crammed into the Music Centre. 'It was chamber music in the true sense of the word, with a very intimate atmosphere,' he said.

For many years the school took full advantage of its position in Scarborough to hear and enjoy a wide variety of music. When the council was subsidising concerts at the Spa there were Bramcote boys in regular attendance. Otherwise they have gone further afield. By 1992, 91 out of the 96 boys in the school were learning a musical instrument and some even two – making well over 100 individual music lessons given each week. Philip Wood, who leaves the school in mid 1993, noted:

'The boys have been kept busy with grade exams, two bands, the choir, various ensembles and groups, IAPS music courses, concerts at the Spa, informal form concerts, the music quiz, boys playing in prayers and much more.

140. Top right: The Music and Arts Centre, with Netherbank behind.
141. Bottom right: John Fuller-Sessions, Sir Marcus Worsley Bt, and John Cundall drinking to the new centre.

When they moved into the centre the art master, Terry Beeston wrote: '. . . and there was light! Or so it seemed in the new art block. There was also warmth, it was clear, spacious and airy, in short an excellent place to practise the arts, and practise we did. The ceramics this year have continued to expand, pottery or pot making gradually giving way to the more imaginative and far more rewarding hand building and sculpting. Chris Leder, after a mammoth struggle (three times) eventually defeated the problems to produce a ceramic figure at work on a potter's wheel. Some say he also defied gravity as the figure decided to move during firing and now seemingly rests in mid-air.

'On the functional side a fine array of table-lamps, mugs, cheese dishes, bowls, jugs and vases now adorn homes around the country. And on the fine arts side the results have once again been rewarding not just personally for the boys but in one instance financially. Anil Bhoomkar, leaving this year for Shrewsbury, gained one of only thirty awards made in the preparatory division of the Public Schools Fine Arts Bursary Fund – The Sir Charles Wheeler Award. This was Bramcote's first entry to these awards . . .' When Terry Beeston left the school in 1989 he described the art facilities there as the ideal teaching situation.

The new centre enabled the art department to develop craft, design and technology. The present art master, Roy Rigley, for instance had some forms in the past few years designing and building model primitive houses. They had to collect suitable materials from Oliver's Mount and the seashore and then construct their models mainly using a 'wattle and daub' technique and no modern adhesives.

142. Roy Rigley with an art class.

143. *Chris Leder's model.*

144. *Donald Dewar and Nick Fuller-Sessions sculpting.*

145. Back in the 1930s it was fun just to lure Oswald Cooper onto the biggest sandcastle built.
146. In the 1970s Hugh Howell-Jones helped the boys develop sandcastle making into a finer art.
147. And in 1987 William Machin, Robert Procopé, James Clive, Henry Starkey and Russell Wilcock walked off with the Sand Sculpting Competition prize held at the South Bay. This was attended by many schools, colleges and individual artists so the boys from Bramcote were delighted to win.

'We wanted to make the school as close to home as possible,' Marion Fuller-Sessions said. Back in 1985, Michael Sutermeister (then 10) found he was in great need of that:

It started with a little rag-around – Hargreaves, Procopé and me. 'Pretend fight,' we called it. I was supposed to be the 'HULK'. I ran at Procopé shouting, 'Hulk will smash you'. I hit him with my chest, and Procopé slid over backwards. I had a quick doubt as I saw Blythe's steel bed-leg. My doubt grew bigger as 'Thud!' Procopé screwed up his face and groaned.

I felt fear, and guilt flew through my mind as I followed the whimpering Procopé along the corridor. I was beginning to whimper too, when Hargreaves shouted, 'He's bleeding!' I saw it too, as blood trickled quickly through the hand Procopé held to the back of his head.

I was very frightened as Mrs Wilson rushed into the bathroom. I asked if there was anything I could do to help. Mrs Wilson pointed to the door, so I waited outside. I felt the fear flow through me as I shivered and tears drifted over my cheeks.

Mr Norris came out of the bathroom. He told me to get washed and into pyjamas, and to come back there. I rushed from the bathroom still shivering. When I came back Mr Norris talked to me in a gentle voice. He had at least some sympathy for me. He told me it was my turn to tidy the form room with Hargreaves.

When I came back Mrs Wilson wanted to see me. I was scared but I had to keep up my courage. I walked into the surgery. Mrs Wilson was quite cross. She showed me Procopé's head, which looked awful, and made me feel worse. I walked into the dorm, wrote my diary and lay there trying to think what it was like from Procopé's point of view. Thoughts filled my mind . . . maybe Procopé would die!

A few minutes later I heard Mrs F-S's voice. I was shivering and very shy. I buried my head in my duvet. Mrs F-S told me to turn over, and she tried to calm me down. After lights out I was attempting to go to sleep . . . Senior boys asked what I was crying for, so someone in the dorm had to go outside and tell them out of my ear-shot. Mr F-S came in and calmed me down. Somehow (I don't know how) but somehow I got to sleep.

In the morning the whole dorm were encouraging me to go and say sorry to Procopé. I saw Procopé's head slip under the covers as I came in. Then the famous words came out of my mouth, 'Sos Procs'.

When the new boys start at the school it is the Medical Matron and her two assistants who make sure they are safe in bed at night – and up in time in the morning. It is to them they turn when they feel ill, or just want to chat. 'It's like a big family,' Lucinda Fisher, the present Medical Matron, said. It's a long day though as they have to take care of the boys' clothes, their health and pastoral care. The Medical Matron also has to be on duty at all home matches.

These days they don't have such major epidemics as in the past, thanks to the availability of vaccinations and antibiotics. Although the *Bramcotian* reported in 1980 that measles went on and on . . . And something like gastric flu can still cause havoc according to the 1975 *Bramcotian*: 'For one brief 24 hour period sickness ran riot through the school. The matrons were awake all night.'

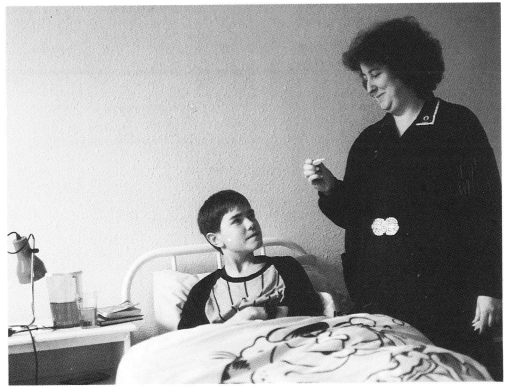

148. *Lucinda Fisher caring for Justin Gregory, February 1993.*

149. John Gerrard with one of the first computers in the Maths Room.

Great leaps forward in the school's history often seem to be almost hidden in *The Bramcotian varia*, as in 1981 when they noted: 'Two micro-computers arrived in the school – a hive of activity in the maths room with John Gerrard in seventh heaven.' The school began steadily to increase the number of computers, the first BBC Model B being bought in 1984. They could even start a club.

'The computer club is normally very interesting,' wrote Jonathan Kealy in 1987 (then aged nine). 'You learn a lot and in the end it is much more fun playing on them when you know how to work them. Mr Vint helps us by putting things on the board and explaining how the computer can help us work out the answers. When I attended the first meeting it was all a bit new to me, as the others were all quite a bit better. After reading a few magazines on computers I got a lot better and understood much more.' Robert Vint then reported:

During the year we have made many additions to our stock of computer equipment, all of which should be compatible with any developments that may occur in the computer department in future years. We now have the use of three BBC Model B Computers, each with disk drive and printer. A new Teletext receiver will enable us to receive computer programmes broadcast by TV stations, and store them on disk. We have also obtained a range of light pens, tracker-balls and joysticks with accompanying educational and graphical software. The word-processor (with spreadsheet for numerical purposes) has proved very popular with the boys for writing letters on.

Three computer groups (for different ability levels) were run during the winter months for those who wished to learn the principles of programming. Boys have produced a range of programs including arithmetic testers, French vocab testers, alphabetical word sorters and various games – not too dramatic when run, but fairly challenging to write.

Finally we are seeing the first signs of computers creeping into subject teaching as Mr

Lundie experiments with his new purchase – a set of computerised weighing scales. This device can display or print graphs of weight change during plant growth, chemical reactions or any other process. Such developments, I am sure, will continue, especially in the maths, science and geography departments, and will be boosted by the emphasis on project and fieldwork in the GCSE.

The BBC Model Bs were replaced in 1988 by eight BBC Master 128s when the old music room was turned into a computer room. Now, instead, of having odd computers scattered throughout the buildings, the school had a fully operational teaching unit along with printers (including a colour one) and a plotter.

In 1992 the parents of those leaving the school that year bought a new IBM compatible computer along with a laser printer and colour scanner. The desk top publishing software made it possible to produce some special effect pages for *The Bramcotian* – now a glossy, professional magazine. James Lundie (science master) commented:

'Perhaps in time we may even be able to typeset *The Bramcotian* in school. This certainly would be a challenge!' As he pointed out: 'We keep up to date with modern themes – in science we have to.' In the late 1980s John Fuller-Sessions warned that there would be more radical changes involving the curriculum. 'The new GCSE exam will have repercussions even at prep school level; the Common Entrance Examination (CEE) is bound to undergo some reform, and our teaching will have to move with these changes. Whatever the distractions, whatever the changes, what goes on in the classroom is still vitally important. It would be easy and tempting to see change as synonymous with progress, to accept the lowering of standards as being kinder and fairer, to be lured by promises of "instant" success.

'There is no substitute for honest, whole-hearted effort. We will keep up with all the necessary changes. We will continue to try to educate boys who enjoy the self-confidence that only comes from knowing that they have at all times done their very best, that they have indeed kept their eye on the ball.

'The Public Schools we use still demand a high standard at CEE and are quite prepared to fail boys who don't reach it. This year, as every year, we had several boys who would not have been successful if they, and the staff who put in many extra hours helping them, had not worked so hard. I am profoundly aware also of the level-headed attitude to the work, and the exams. Boys remain cheerful, they carry on their "extras", they play in matches; no one becomes twitchy, pale or nervous, except perhaps the headmaster!'

Project work was now included in the CEE and the topics covered for the extended science papers in 1987 included *A Comparison of Seashore Flora and Fauna*; *Water and Acid Rain* and *Bacteria and Antibiotics*. James Lundie noted:

'These projects gave the boys a chance to go into a particular subject area in some depth and they all seemed to enjoy the challenge of the work. The finished projects were of a very high standard and a credit to each one of them.' And in 1989 he wrote:

'It was with a certain degree of apprehension that I first opened the final version of the National Curriculum for science. After an initial study of the document I have come to a number of conclusions. The main one is that we in the prep school world are lucky to have an already established tradition of science teaching. All our boys learn science from the word go in a laboratory, something that is very rare in primary schools. Moreover they are taught by science specialists, which must give them a better grounding in the subject at an earlier age. Further reading of the details of the actual topics lead me to think that the National Curriculum has taken some of its ideas from the philosophy of the Common Entrance syllabus . . .' (Jim Hornby would have been pleased!)

Geography fieldwork projects were required for the first time in 1988 and several boys spent many hours studying the processes of erosion by the sea on the cliffs of the South Bay. Robert Vint reported that the boys used the word processors to great advantage, to produce highly professional tables, text and graphs and added:

'I feel that the project has been very worthwhile and that its inclusion in the CEE has worked to the benefit of those boys who panic or work slowly in exams but know their work thoroughly.' In following years the boys often made modern geographical studies of local shopping centres. The teaching of maths also had to undergo changes so that the boys would be more prepared for the new-style GCSE exams when they were at Public School.

Most prep schools organise special outings for the 'leavers' once the CE Examinations are over. Bramcote did likewise for most of the 1970s and 1980s but in 1987 they inaugurated what has become a unique feature of the school – a full leavers' programme. Richard Lytle, the main organiser of this, explained:

By lunchtime on the Wednesday of CEE week, when most of the candidates are punch-drunk with the problem of Maths II, whether or not embarrass has one or two Rs, and what Henry III's dates were, the leavers' programme is announced.

At first sight this looks like a four week jolly, a sort of Bramcote Butlins during which the mind can drift off into neutral or hedonism rules – and yes, it's true that the month is designed to be fun. But lurking in some of the tasks, projects and activities are all sorts of challenges of both a physical and a mental nature. Take *pontoon* for example – this is an on-running 'individual' competition which often involves teamwork. Random teams are drawn for each task, individual scores determined by where the team finishes. Some of the *pontoon* activities are straightforward games, such as five-a-side football or hockey, but there is also a trivial pursuit match – and the initiative tests. In these all sorts of things are tested; the ability to work together, the ability to think quickly and logically, to listen to the ideas of those not necessarily regarded as being clever – the ability to sift out the impractical. A new test, devised this year, gave a group of six a canoe, various bits of rope, two pieces of plank and a step-ladder – with which they had to reach a small jar of liquid attached to the middle of the swimming pool roof.

Another on-running feature of the programme is the mythical £10,000 with which pairs play on the stock market. The initial buy has to involve at least five companies and dealing charges are fixed at a minimum of £20 or one per cent. The winning group this year (1989) made a profit of £700.

The leavers' programme also includes craft, design and technology (CDT) and modern technology and computer sections. One of their CDT projects in 1990 was to design, make a model and cost the M3 extension, the Winchester bypass. How much they considered Maurice Platnauer's wishes is not known. The main physical test of the leavers' programme is still the Bramcote Walk.

150. Oliver Hudson rests his sore feet before continuing the Bramcote Walk.

151. Top left: John DePree, a 1990 leaver, getting expert tuition at Staxton Wold.
152. Bottom left: The 1992 leavers – Richard Hall, Charles Hall, Tim Jones, Nicholas Clark, Richard Hardie, Richard Bennett and James Alton, with Jack Wilson kneeling – all ready for some paint balling near York.
153. Below: Major Johnny Howard-Vyse organised the trip to the Royal Artillery at Attenbrooke Barracks in 1990 – and his own son, James, got a chance to join in too.

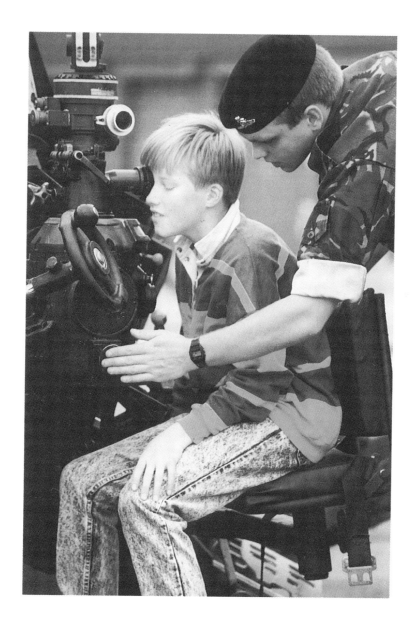

Bramcote School
July 1991
(For the last time!)

Dear All,

My last letter from Bramcote! Anyway, I am going to tell you a bit more about the Bramcote Walk. It starts and finishes at the School. There are six major hills and the normal length is 36 miles plus any necessary detours (I did 38 miles). It goes along the coast for about eight miles, then along a disused railway line, in a big circle through Forestry Commission land. You have three main stops for meals – breakfast, lunch and tea. You set out at about 7.30 am and arrive back at about 8.00 pm. Breakfast is at 10.15, lunch at 1.30 and tea at 5.00. The walk is on the same day as Cayton Bay. I went water-skiing the day before yesterday. I managed to ski quite well and I managed five seconds holding on by just one hand!! (Then I fell off!)

We also went to Beverley races, and had a competition with play money which our team came first. I made a net profit of 2p on my small bets with a bookie, thanks to a horse called Mendoso. I spent all the winnings except 2p on other horses!

Our group did cooking a few days ago. We did melon and black grape cocktail, paella with green salad, and bananas poached in cider or Tipsy strawberries. All at a cost of less than £2.50 per head. We also visited the Coke factory at Wakefield, biggest in the world. They have six lines, three for bottles and three for cans, churning out six million cans and one million bottles per day. It was all incredibly automated and amazingly well designed.

11.06 – I have just come out of the service, which this week was run by the leavers. We had: Exciting Hymns, One lesson, No Psalm, A long sermon, A small play (in which I acted a baby). I bet that the whole of the school will be humming the hymn tunes for weeks. It was much more fun than a normal service.

I hope Mum enjoyed Mothers' Day – I certainly did! Afterwards we had a film, just like on Saturday nights.

Gervase Markham

As the boys were granted more freedoms (like being able to go into town) and corporal punishment was gradually phased out new systems of discipline within the school had to be found. By the mid-1980s the need to evolve a new communications system which would break down the old 'them and us' attitudes between boys and masters became urgent. For the first time the school set up a full prefects system with the emphasis on finding those who were mature enough and had the strength of character to go to the staff and discuss problems – without actually 'sneaking' on specific boys. Diana Gerrard who was at the school in the 1970s was very aware of the gulf then between the staff and boys. In fact, she felt she had more problems because her parents were teaching there than by being one of the first girls in the school. There was also the gulf between the juniors and the seniors, often as a direct result of the senior boys being held responsible for certain areas of school discipline and being able to give punishments like running round the field. Mary Gerrard (who teaches maths and divinity) commented:

I think the prefect's job now is very much a caring one. When we have the prefects' meeting we discuss with them whether the boys are unhappy, if the boys are being teased or whether perhaps there is a boy who is a little bit homesick. We would also discuss with them if somebody is being a nuisance. When we first came the senior boys were expected to discipline the younger ones to a certain degree. I didn't like it because I didn't think a 13-year-old had the judgement to tell when an eight-year-old was being naughty – an eight-year-old's natural bounciness could appear to be naughtiness when it wasn't. And there was bound to creep in to this type of punishment a kind of bullying which was very unfortunate. The result was far less friendliness between the senior boys and the younger ones. These days I find even the smallest boys mixing with the senior boys.

When we first came punishment was a lot more physical. If you were caught out of bed in the dormitory you got the slipper. If the staff found you were late for something you were sent to run around the field. Now there is more talking to the boys and trying to find punishments that fit the crime which requires more hard work from the staff. You have to spend a lot more time with a child when he has misbehaved because you are trying to talk him through it and perhaps find him something to do which helps him realise that what he has done is anti-social. I think there is more awareness amongst the boys that if there is some form of anti-social behaviour it affects the other children and they are more prepared to talk about it. If a boy has been naughty he might come to me of an evening and talk his way through a day and try to sort out any problems.

The Form Masters meet with them every Saturday morning and give them a chance to air any grievances. We are always open to suggestions and we do encourage the boys to say if they feel they are being treated unfairly. They are encouraged to feel they can come to us if there is a problem.

Her husband, John, worked with John Fuller-Sessions to create weekly prefects' meetings which were relaxed and open and where various problems in the school could be discussed and resolved. They also sought to improve the channels of communication with the other staff, with frequent 'natter sessions' as well as regular staff meetings. This included maintaining a high standard of academic work whilst encouraging all the various activities. John Gerrard spoke of the major role John and Marion Fuller-Sessions played in the 'gentling' of the system and how, in the three years since the Fuller-Sessions left he and his wife

had sought to develop and further establish this. Of himself he said:

'I too am very concerned that we should not lose our academic reputation. It is a great credit to a wonderfully dedicated staff that the boys now enjoy such a diversity of interests and opportunities, but with so much time and energy devoted to extra-curricular activity and excursions in the evenings and at weekends, we have to strive all the harder to maintain the standards of scholastic purpose and endeavour for which the school has been renowned.' Peter Terry commented:

'On the academic side Bramcote has maintained an extremely high standard (with six scholarships between March and May 1991) so with all the extra activities they have kept up educational standards.' When Bramcote was inspected in May 1992 under the provisions of the Children Act 1989 it was reported that the school did not have a clear statement of how control was maintained and how sanctions were used to tackle unacceptable behaviour. The report[1] stated:

It is in the area of personal relationships that Bramcote's way of life is especially remarkable. The prospectus states that 'discipline is achieved through understanding and cooperation' and makes reference to 'a friendly and tolerant atmosphere'. It is the view of the inspecting officer that these aims are indeed achieved.

In group discussion boys found it quite difficult to describe the concept of 'punishment' within the school. Acceptance of reasonable conduct as the norm rather than the exception is well understood and appreciated. Lapses in these standards are primarily dealt with by discussion, but may lead to minor sanctions of very short duration.

So well established is this ethos, that until the time of the inspection there was no statement published concerning discipline other than the passages in the prospectus. A simple additional statement has now been produced.

The Inspector found that corporal punishment had not been administered for a number of years and that in no circumstances did sanctions involve the restriction of a child's liberty. (In October 1992 the Governors formally recognised that corporal punishment was no longer used in the school.) The Inspector concluded:

It is absolutely clear that the well-being of children, in every aspect of their lives – social, emotional and educational – is an over-riding concern to every adult within the school. The inspecting officer spoke with people on the domestic and ground staff, all of whom reflected this approach. The "whole boy" is indeed the concern of everyone.

When this and the present curriculum is compared with the 1948 report prepared by HM Inspectors it is obvious just how much Bramcote has opened the door to the future. But then one looks back on those long lost photographs of Samuel Servington Savery and the sight of Pidcock carrying a boy on his shoulders at Cayton Bay and there is a strong sense of continuity: of pride and joy in 'their boys' – together with a determination to equip the boys in the best way they could for the world the leavers would meet outside.

[1] Report of Mr P. Major, Registration and Inspection Officer, under the provisions of the Children Act 1989, for NYCC Social Services Department.

Bramcote School Headmasters

1893–1911   Sir Samuel Servington Savery M.P.

1909–1945   R.G. Pidcock
with R.D. Slater   1909–1925

1930–1957   O. Cooper
with A.Urling-Smith   1945–1946
with F.M. Hamerton   1945–1968
with A.D. Stow   1954–1955

1954–1967   J.W. Hornby

1967–1969   J.M. Coates

1968–1983   C.S. McGarrigle

1972–1990   J.F. Fuller-Sessions

1985–   J.R. Gerrard

1992–   J.G.W. Walker

APPENDIX 2

Chairmen of Governors

1957–1970   O. Cooper

1970–1980   E.E. Sabben-Clare

1980–1988   J.A. Cundall

1988–1991   His Honour Judge John Lord

1991–   R.D. Marshall

Jeremy Ware sent the following list of those who have studied at Bramcote School and who were descended either from his grandparents, John and Sophie Ware, or from his wife's grandparents, Mr and Mrs Wright of Ferriby:

H.A. Ware
J.W.Ware
Jeremy Ware
William Ware
Julian Ware
Henry Ware
Maylin Ware

R.R.Ware
Joseph Gibson
Henry Gibson
Andrew Gibson
Stephen Hollins-Gibson
William Hollins-Gibson
Nicholas Sandford

The Wrights:

Maylin Wright
Willie Wright
Edward Wright
Jonathon Wright
Roderick Wright
Timothy Wright

Quentin Wright
John Robinson
David Robinson
Hugh Robinson
Dominic Robinson (whose stepbrother was also at Bramcote).

APPENDIX 4

Dulce et decorum est pro patria mori.

Addy, J. C.	02-05	Capt. 10th East Yorks. (May 3, 1917) M.C.
Atkinson, G.J.B.	02-08	Lieut. Dorset R. (June 19, 1915).
Anderton, G.E.A.	05-09	Lieut. M.G.C. attd. Lancs. Fus. Despatches. (March 22, 1918).
Bagshawe, G.H.	02-04	2nd Lt. 1st Dragoons. (May 13, 1915).
Brodrick-English, J.F.	01-06	L-Cpl. 1/5 Seaforth Highrs. (April 21, 1917).
Burdekin, G.E.	04-06	2nd Lt. 3rd Notts & Derby (Sherwood Foresters). (Jan 26, 1915).
Carr, S.T.	06-11	Lieut. 11th Manchesters. (Sept. 26, 1916).
Carver, G.H. (see Bagshawe)		
Childe, D.F.	07-10	Lieut. York & Lancs. (Dec. 19, 1915).
Cranswick, G.A.	11-12	2nd Lt. York & Lancs., attd. R.F.C. (Missing Nov. 18, 1917).
Graham, H.C.	00-01	2nd Lt. 9th Yorks. R. (Oct. 1, 1917).
Graham, M.H.	06-09	Lieut. 3rd attd. 1st Yorks. R. (June 15, 1915).
Hicking, F.J.	09-11	2nd Lt. W. Yorks. (July 1, 1916).
Jepson, A.G.L.	03-04	Capt. 1st City of London R.F. (Sept. 15, 1916). Despatches.
Kempson, J.R.	05-07	Midshipman R.N. (Drowned in Hawke, Oct. 14, 1914).
Mackay, P.S.	05-11	2nd Lt. K.O.S.B. (April 14, 1917).
Mitchell, J.S.	06-10	2nd Lt. R.F.C. (Oct. 5, 1916).
Paul, G.G.	02-08	Lieut. 2nd Dragoon Guards. (Oct. 31, 1914).
Richardson, W.Q.N.	10-12	2nd Lt. R.F.C. (Oct. 6, 1917).
Salter, J.H.R.	07-12	2nd Lt. 3rd E.Yorks & R.F.C. (Oct. 13, 1917).
Schute, J.H.	02-06	Lieut. 6th Royal Irish Fusiliers. (August 15, 1915).
Spendlove, G.T.	06-09	
Tindall, R.F.	98-99	2nd Lt. 2nd Lincolns. (Sept. 25, 1915).
Tindall, E.V.	99	2nd Lt. 2nd K.R.R. (Oct. 10, 1914).
Tolson, J.M.	07-12	2nd Lt. R.F.A. (Oct. 20, 1918).
Walker, R.F.	03-08	2nd Lt. 2nd Manchesters. (Oct. 21, 1914).
Ware, J.W.	08-11	2nd Lt. R.E. (July 11, 1916).

Members of the Staff

Abbott, L.P.	14	2nd Lt. 7th Leicesters. (July 14, 1916).
Callinan, T.W.	09-11	Lieut. Durham L.I. (April 1915).
de Reuter, H.J.	06	Private Black Watch. (Nov. 13, 1916).

Pro aris et focis

Ackroyd, W.	00-02	Lieut. Royal Dragoons. Wounded May 13, 1915.
Addy, R.	02-05	Capt. 16th E. Yorks.
Alleyne, Sir J.M., Bart.	99-04	Lieut. R.N., H.M.S. Lord Clive D.S.C.
Alleyne, R.M.	02-04	Lieut. R.N., H.M.S. New Zealand.
Allott, A.D.	00-05	2nd Lt. Indian Army (Cavalry).
Arliss, H.T.S.	04-08	Lieut. R.N.
Ash, E.C.	01-02	2nd Lt. R.F.A. Wounded Oct. 11, 1917.
Ash, S.H.	02-03	Major R.E.
Barker, Rev. T.H.W.	96-01	Capt., Chaplain to the Forces.
Barmby, A.J.W.	03-04	Capt. West Yorks. Despatches.
Batty, E.D.M.	04-10	Lieut. 201st Siege Battery, R.G.A.
Bedwell, F.C.	01-07	Capt. G.S.O. 3. Despatches.
Bedwell, T.G.	05-08	Lieut. R.N.D. Prisoner of War in Holland.
Bedwell, E.P.	07-10	Leading Telegraphist (wireless), R.N.
Bell, F.	99-03	Capt. R.E. Wounded twice. Despatches M.C.
Berry, W.	01-02	Major 8th W. Yorks. Invalided home, Dec., 1915.
Bladworth, K.T.	09-11	Private H.A.C.
Bladworth, C.J.	10-11	Private H.A.C.
Bolckow, H.C.R.	07-10	2nd Lt. 7th Dragoon Guards.
Broadbent, A.V.	05-10	Lt. (temp. Capt.), 5th W. Riding R. Wounded twice. M.C.
Burton, R.W.	99-03	Lieut. M.G.C. Wounded. Despatches. M.C.
Burton, R.C.	01-05	Lieut. A.S.C., attd. 5th Middlesex.
Burton, R.T.	04-06	Capt. Coldstream Guards. Wounded.
Burton, C.R.	07-10	Capt. (Tank commander), 7th Tank Corps.
Byass, A.	97-98	Capt. A.S.C. M.C.
Cadman, P.A.	06-12	Cadet, Cavalry Cadet School, Netheravon.
Clifford, E.C.	97-99	Major R.F.A. M.C.
Cooper, W.G.L.	09-13	Midshipman R.N., H.M.S. Revenge.
Cox, J.H.	99-01	Corporal I.W.T. R.E.
Cox, A.N.	99-05	Private M.T.S., 6th Canadian R. Troops.
Cox, R.N.	04-09	Lieut. 2nd Essex R.
Cradock-Watson, K.	11-14	Cadet R.M.C., Sandhurst.
Davies, S.	00-03	Lieut. 9th Durham L.I.
Dixon, C.	99-02	Sergeant R.F.C.
Dobinson, H.	00-05	Lieut. R.F.A. Wounded twice. M.C.
Dodsworth, L.L.S.	97-04	Lieut. 12th West Yorks. Wounded. Invalided out May 1917.
Dougall, N.S.	10-11	Lieut. R.F.C. Wounded Nov. 17, 1915.
Drawbridge, W.N.	09-12	Midshipman R.N. H.M.S. Iron Duke.

Dunlop, D.M.	04-06	Capt. Seaforth Highrs. Wounded Sept. 25, 1915.
Empson, C.E.R.	08-13	Midshipman R.N. H.M.S. Neptune.
Eyre, W.R.P.	02-04	Lieut. R.N. H.M.S. Weymouth.
Farrer, R.N.	98-00	Capt. R.A.M.C.
Fennell, G.W.P.	07-12	RMA Woolwich
Field, G.W.	98-00	Lieut. 6th Worcesters, attd. M.G.C.
Firth, A.M.B.	99	Capt. 4th York & Lancs.
Fisher, G.H.	09-13	2nd Lt. R.F.A.
Fitz-Gibbon, A.F.G.	01-03	Lieut. 81st Sikh Pioneers. M.C.
Fitz-Gibbon, D.F.G.	01-03	Flt. Capt. R.N. D.S.C.
Gaunt, A.	00-03	Lieut. Australian M.C.
Gibb, R.	99-01	With the Friends' Ambulance unit in France.
Gibb, P.	99-01	Capt. 4th Army Troop Supply. M.C.
Gibb, E.A.	01-02	Naval Surgeon.
Gothorp, W.Y.	10-14	2nd Lt R.A.F.
Gregory, D.A.	08-13	Cadet R.F.A., Exeter.
Griffith, W.G.A.	09-12	2nd Lt. Sherwood Foresters.
Hardy, J.C.	97-00	Sapper R.E.
Hardy, V.C.	06-08	Capt. Northumberland Fus. Wounded and prisoner, May 12, 1915.
Hardy, A.C.	06-10	Capt. Northern Cyclist Bn.
Harrowing, W.W.	08-12	2nd Lt. 1st Duke of Cornwall's L.I.
Hern, J.R.B.	08-11	2nd Lt. R.F.A.
Hewetson, R.P.	00-03	Capt. R.F.A. Wounded Jan. 3, 1918.
Hill, C.L.	04-09	Capt. 8th Sherwood Foresters.
Hirst, G.A.W.	04-08	2nd Lt. 1st County of London Yeomanry.
Hitchcock, C.G.	98-02	Capt. R.A.M.C.
Hudson, H.C.H.	95-98	Lieut. 12th Hussars
Hunter, G.M.T.S.	02-04	Lieut. King's African Rifles.
Illingworth, H.C.H.	06-08	Capt. K.R.R. Wounded taken prisoner Feb. 28, 1917. Interned in Switzerland. M.C.
Jessop, T.	97-99	Major 1st Lincs Yeomanry
Jessup, G.S.	94-01	Corpl. 1st Lincs. Yeomanry, attd. Imperial Camel Bgde.
Joblin, B.E.	07-09	2nd Lt. Labour Corps.
Jones, O.S.	02-04	2nd Lt. 16th Middlesex. Invalided out.
Jowitt, R.L.P.	09-13	Private, Inns of Court O.T.C.
Kebbell, F.H.	97-99	
Kempson, W.R.	00-06	Capt. R.F.A., attd. R.N.A.S. Croix de Guerre.
Kitching, J.E.	96	Capt. R.E. Despatches.
Kitson, G.H.	05-10	Lieut. R.F.A. Wounded May 12, 1917.
Kitson, G.L.	07-12	2nd Lt. R.F.A.
Kitson-Clark, E.B.	09-11	Sub-Lieut. R.N. H.M.S. Tigress. T.B.D.

Lambert, H.G.	06-11	2nd Lt. R.F.A.
Learoyd, P.C.	07-11	Lieut. R.F.A.
Leng, D.C.	98-04	Capt. 1/1 Queen's Own Yorkshire Dragoons.
Longbottom, W.E.	07-12	2nd Lt. 3rd Dragoon Guards.
Lucas, S.	06-10	Capt. 3rd York & Lancs. Wounded three times. 1914 Star.
Lyon, W.E.	98-00	Capt. 19th Royal Hussars. Despatches.
Mackay, A.H.	00-02	Capt. A.S.C.
Mackay, K.	00-04	Capt. 1/5 W. Yorks. M.C.
Mackay, D.S.	03-07	Lieut. Queen's Own Yorkshire Dragoons, transf. Indian Cavalry.
Mackay, R.P.	05-07	Private York & Lancs. Discharged, medically unfit.
Master, E.S.	09-13	Cadet, R.M.C., Sandhurst.
Maynard, G.E.	99-04	Paymaster R.N.
McCraith, K.Y.	01-04	Capt. 7th Sherwood Foresters. Wounded Oct. 13, 1915.
McEwan, A.G.	04-08	Lieut. R.N. H.M.S. Agamemnon.
Middleton, A.L.	03-06	Capt. R.F.A. Invalided home 1916.
Middleton, A.J.	04-08	Lieut. R.F.A. Wounded Oct. 12, 1917. M.C.
Miller, F.C.	03-07	Lieut. R.N.
Monkman, G.B.	04-09	Lieut. 18th Manchesters, transf. R.F.C.
Moore, J.L.	10-13	2nd Lt. Duke of Wellington's W. Riding R.
Naylor, P.	99-04	Sapper and Despatch Rider. 102nd Canadians. Missing May 1918.
Nunneley, G.A.	06-07	Lieut. R.N. H.M.S. Inflexible.
Paul, A.S.	05-10	Lieut. 2nd Dragoon Guards.
Peacocke, L.G.L.	05-08	Lieut. King's Dragoon Guards.
Pearson, T.S.	05-07	Lieut. R.F.A., attd. R.F.C. M.C.
Pease, E.G.	05-06	Lieut. 15th (The King's) Hussars.
Phillips, C.J.H.	02-07	Capt. R.F.A.
Platnauer, M.	98-01	Capt. & Adj. R.F.A.
Priestman, J.L.	02-05	Capt. (acting) R.F.A. M.C.
Pritchard, R.T.	07-12	2nd Lieut. K.O.S.B.
Proctor, S.R.	06-09	2nd Lt. R.F.C.
Reynolds, L.	94-97	2nd Lt. Tank Corps.
Reynolds, C.	96	Capt. 49th divisional train, A.S.C.
Rogers, P.M.	08-09	2nd Lt. R.F.C.
Salter, G.C.T.	07-11	Lieut. 1st E. Yorks and Tank Corps, transf. R.F.C. M.C.
Schute, F.G.	99-05	Capt. 4th Royal Irish Fusiliers.
Shepheard-Walwyn, R.F.	09-10	Capt. Tank Corps.
Shepherd, L.G.	97-02	2nd Lt. 7th Durham L.I.
Smith, J.T.	04-08	Air Mechanic R.F.C.

Spinks, I.	93-94	Bombardier R.G.A.
Statter, W.A.S.	98-01	Capt. Intelligence Staff, War Office.
Stephenson, E.V.	06-09	Capt. R.F.A. (special reserve).
Storry, F.R.C.	08-12	Cadet O.C.B., Newton Ferrers.
Thompson, G.L.	06-10	2nd Lt. R.F.A.
Thomson, E.B.	05-10	Lieut. R.F.A.
Thomson, A.J.	05-12	2nd Lt. R.F.A.
Tolson, E.A.	01-05	
Turner, G. McD.	95-02	Flt. Commander R.F.C.
Turton, G.A.	06-09	Capt. R.F.C.
Tyzack, R.	07-10	Flt. Sub-Lieut. R.N.A.S.
Tyzack, B.	07-10	2nd Lt. R.F.A.
Vaile, J.P.	95-97	Signaller R.G.A.
Vickers, C.G.	06-08	Capt. 7th (Robin Hood) Sherwood Foresters Wounded Oct. 14, 1915. V.C.
Waddington, R.M.	99-02	Capt. 8th W. Yorks. Wounded twice.
Waistell, A.M.	98-02	Lieut. R.F.C. Wounded.
Wallis, J.D.	99-04	2nd Lt. Argyll & Sutherland Highrs. Prisoner in Bulgaria May 8, 1917.
Wallis, C.T.	04-08	Sub-lieut. R.N.
Wallis, T.G.	08-12	Cadet R.F.A.
Ward, H.G.L.	03-10	Capt. 2nd Worcesters. Wounded twice.
Warwick, D.V.	02-04	Major 59th Battery R.F.A.
Warwick, J.C.G.	07-08	Lieut. 1/1 South Notts. Hussars.
Watts, A.W.	99-00	2nd Lt. 26th Liverpool R. Invalided out June 1917.
Wilkinson, M.	08-11	2nd Lieut. A.S.C.
Wilson, Arnold	95-99	Capt. 1/8 W. Yorks. Invalided home April 1915.
Wilson, Alan	02-04	Lieut. R.F.A.
Woodruff, W.L.	06-11	2nd Lt. 211 Trench Mortar Battery, attd. R.F.A.
Yewdall, C.D.	98-01	Lieut. R.F.A.

Members of the Staff

Bell, E.A.	09	Lieut. (T.F.) O.C. Giggleswick O.T.C.
Holliday, R.J.M.	00-04	Naval Instructor R.N.
Ling, G.A.	04-08	Lieut. Suffolks. Wounded April 28, 1917. Resigned Commission.
Usher, T.	14	Capt. 9th Suffolks.
Young, D.	14	Major King's Royal Rifles. Wounded August 1915.
Pidcock, R.G. Joint Headmaster		2nd Lt. K.R.R.

Appendix

Those who died from 1939-1945

C.H.M. Appleton, H.A.D. Barber, J.R. Boissier, G.J. D'Arcy Clark, J.P.W.H. Davis, G.A. Dawson, J.B. Dunlop, M.T. Edwards, G.C. Frew, J. Geldard, A.P.J. Grundy, M.G. Ham, D.H.W. Hanson, D. Hellyer, P.J.D. Hoyle, R.D. Hutton-Squire, J. Ives, E.P.C. Kidd, R.F. Kipling, J. Knapp, M.G. Lillingston, J.L. Machin, A.L. Mather, A.R.H. Maynard, H.A. Paton, R.B. Paver-Crow, W.U. Ritson, I.M. Robertson-Walker, R.A. Smallwood, R.H. Stephenson, K.T.P. Terry, W.I.E. Thorburn.

APPENDIX 5

School Honours

July	1901	M. PLATNAUER, Open Classical Scholarship at Shrewsbury School.
July	1902	P. GARDNER-SMITH, Mathematical Scholarship at Wakefield Grammar School.
July	1902	P. GARDNER-SMITH, Open Scholarship at Sherborne School.
Mar	1904	J.M. ALLEYNE, Naval Cadetship in the Britannia.
June	1904	R.M. ALLEYNE, Naval Cadetship at Osborne.
June	1904	W.P.EYRE, Naval Cadetship at Osborne.
Mar	1905	P.O'B. GIBSON, Open Classical Scholarship at Shrewsbury.
Mar	1905	W.R. KEMPSON, Open Classical Scholarship at Rossall.
June	1905	H. ROBINSON, Open Mathematical Scholarship at Repton.
June	1906	W.R. KEMPSON, Open Mathematical Scholarship at Repton.
Dec	1906	R.T. BURTON, Naval Cadetship at Osborne.
Dec	1906	D.M. DUNLOP, Naval Cadetship at Osborne.
July	1907	A.G. NUNNELEY, Naval Cadetship at Osborne.
Dec	1907	F.C. MILLER, Naval Cadetship at Osborne.
Mar	1908	J.T. SMITH, Open Classical Scholarship at Shrewsbury.
Mar	1908	R.F. WALKER, First Mathematical Scholarship at Shrewsbury.
Mar	1908	H.T.S. ARLISS, Naval Cadetship at Osborne.
June	1908	C.T. WALLIS, Naval Cadetship at Osborne.
June	1908	C.G. VICKERS, Open Scholarship at Oundle.
Dec	1908	T.G. BEDWELL, Naval Cadetship at Osborne.
June	1909	E.P.K. HOUGH, First Open Scholarship at Repton.
Dec	1910	C.R. BURTON, Naval Cadetship at Osborne.
July	1911	J.W. WARE, 3rd on Winchester Election Roll.
July	1911	M. WILKINSON, 23rd on Winchester Election Roll.
July	1911	P.S. MACKAY, 1st Scholarship at Sedbergh.
July	1911	E.B. CLARK, Naval Cadetship at Osborne.
Dec	1911	M. WILKINSON, 1st Classical Scholarship at Haileybury.
Dec	1911	R.B. ATKINSON, Classical Scholarship at Haileybury.
July	1912	W.G.A. GRIFFITH, 2nd Scholarship at Sedbergh.
Nov	1912	G.W.P. FENNELL, 3rd Scholarship at Haileybury.
Mar	1913	C.E.R. EMPSON, Naval Cadetship at Osborne.
July	1913	W.G.L. COOPER, Naval Cadetship at Osborne.
July	1915	E.D.C. ROSE, 4th Scholarship at Oundle.
July	1915	L.H. CRADOCK-WATSON, 3rd Scholarship at Sherborne.
Nov	1915	C.D. WILKINSON, 1st Scholarship at Haileybury.
Dec	1915	R.H. PARKER, Naval Cadetship at Osborne.
Mar	1916	J.L. MACHIN, Naval Cadetship at Osborne.
Dec	1916	J.M. SMALLWOOD, Naval Cadetship at Osborne.
Dec	1916	J.E.H. MASON, Naval Cadetship at Osborne.
July	1917	J.G. BEEVOR, 2nd on Winchester Election Roll.

July	1917	A.J.E. SEALY, 5th on Winchester Election Roll.
July	1917	J.W. BROOKS, 12th on Winchester Election Roll.
July	1917	R.R. WARE, 15th on Winchester Election Roll.
July	1917	T.B. RENDEL, Naval Cadetship at Osborne.
Dec	1917	E.E.A. LANE, 3rd Foundation Scholarship at Marlborough.
Mar	1918	A.G. CLARKE, Naval Cadetship at Osborne.
June	1919	C.C. COBB, 18th on Winchester Election Roll.
Dec	1919	R.H. STEPHENSON, Naval Cadetship at Osborne.
Dec	1919	A.N.F. WEBB, Naval Cadetship at Osborne.
June	1920	C.C. COBB, 2nd on Winchester Election Roll.
July	1921	S.G.L. TURNBULL, Naval Cadetship at Dartmouth.
Dec	1921	C.G. CAFFIN, (left April 1921) Scholarship at Wellington College.
Mar	1922	C.M.H. GLOVER, 2nd Scholarship at Shrewsbury.
June	1922	R.D. HUTTON-SQUIRE, Scholarship at Charterhouse.
June	1922	J.M.C. CLAYTON, 3rd Scholarship at Lancing.
June	1922	M. DU PRE COOPER, 12th on Winchester Election Roll.
June	1922	R.H. THORNLEY, 19th on Winchester Election Roll.
Nov	1922	M.G. LILLINGSTON, Scholarship at Wellington College.
Dec	1922	D.F. WEBB, Naval Cadetship at Dartmouth.
Mar	1923	R.M. HORNSBY, 5th Scholarship at Shrewsbury.
Mar	1923	G.F.W. TURNBULL, Naval Cadetship at Dartmouth.
June	1923	R.H. THORNLEY, 7th on Winchester Election Roll.
June	1924	A.M. RENDEL, 7th Scholarship at Rugby.
June	1924	A.J. HUTTON-SQUIRE, 4th Scholarship at Charterhouse.
June	1924	G.W. MARKHAM, 19th (Exhibitioner) on Winchester Election Roll.
June	1925	G.C. WRIGLEY, 4th Scholarship at Uppingham.
June	1925	W.J.E. PHILLIPS, 6th Scholarship at Malvern.
June	1925	J.M.S. TULLOCH, Exhibition at Oundle
July	1925	A.S. WHITWORTH, Naval Cadetship at Dartmouth.
Nov	1925	H.D. BARTON, Scholarship at Wellington College.
Nov	1925	E.P.C. KIDD, Scholarship at Wellington College.
June	1926	R.A. IRVING, 5th on Winchester Election Roll.
Nov	1926	D.L. CLEMENTS, Scholarship at Haileybury College.
Dec	1926	R.F. KIPLING, Naval Cadetship at Dartmouth.
Mar	1927	J.A.V. HICKLEY, Naval Cadetship at Dartmouth.
June	1927	J.V. WILKINSON, 6th Foundation Scholarship at Marlborough College.
July	1927	J.V. WILKINSON, Naval Cadetship at Dartmouth.
June	1928	J.M.F. NORRIS, 17th (Exhibitioner) on Winchester Election Roll.
Dec	1928	J.A. PHILLIPS, Naval Cadetship at Dartmouth.
May	1929	V.J. WRIGLEY, 2nd Scholarship at Uppingham.
June	1929	J.H. HUMPHREY, 1st on Winchester Election Roll.
June	1929	D.A. LLOYD, 5th Scholarship at Sherborne.
Mar	1930	C.W. WRIGHT, Townsend-Warner History Prize (1st).
June	1930	C.W. WRIGHT, 2nd Scholarship at Charterhouse.
June	1930	C.N.F. NORRIS, 4th on Winchester Election Roll.

Dec 1930 A.P. WILKINSON, Naval Cadetship at Dartmouth.
May 1931 C.P.C. DE WESSELOW, 6th on Winchester Election Roll.
May 1931 C.G.D. SWINNERTON, 9th on Winchester Election Roll.
June 1931 E.V. WRIGHT, Townsend-Warner History Prize (3rd).
June 1931 E.V. WRIGHT, 2nd Scholarship at Charterhouse.
Dec 1931 I.M. ROBERTSON-WALKER, Naval Cadetship at Dartmouth.
Mar 1932 R.A. PEEBLES-BROWN, Honorary Scholarship at Shrewsbury.
June 1932 R.A. TURTON, 2nd Scholarhip at Uppingham.
July 1932 M.W. DICK, Townsend-Warner History Prize (1st)
July 1932 I.R. MACKRILL, Townsend-Warner History Prize (5th)
May 1933 A.P.J. GRUNDY, 6th Scholarship at Shrewsbury.
June 1933 M.W. DICK, 1st on Winchester Election Roll.
June 1933 J.B. HASTED, 12th on Winchester Election Roll.
July 1933 D.V. BALDWIN, 5th Scholarship at Stowe.
July 1933 M.W. DICK, Townsend-Warner History Prize (2nd).
June 1934 E.J. HUDSON, 9th Foundation Scholarship at Marlborough.
Dec 1935 D.B. HOLDSWORTH, Naval Cadetship at Dartmouth.
June 1936 R.M. HONE, 2nd on Winchester Election Roll.
June 1937 R.D. CAMPBELL, 1st Scholarship at Shrewsbury.
June 1938 J.K.B. ILLINGWORTH, 1st on Winchester Election Roll.
June 1938 D.L. STEWART, 3rd Foundation Scholarship at Marborough.
June 1938 G.H. BLAIR, (left July 1937), 3rd Scholarship at Fettes.
June 1939 J.W. BLAIR, 3rd Scholarship at Fettes.
June 1939 T. WHEILDON BROWN, 8th Scholarship at Clifton.
Dec 1939 M.S. BOISSIER, Naval Cadetship at Dartmouth.
June 1940 B.J. REYNOLDS, 11th Scholarship at Rugby.
June 1940 J.N. REDFERN, 4th Scholarship at Oundle.
June 1940 M. MAYNARD, 13th (Exhibitioner) on Winchester Election Roll.
June 1940 G.R. EDWARDS, 20th (Exhibitioner) on Winchester Election Roll.
June 1940 T.S. ZEALLEY, 4th Scholarship at Sherborne.
Dec 1940 M.H. GEM, Naval Cadetship at Dartmouth.
June 1941 J.G. ROBINSON, 3rd Scholarship at Rugby.
Nov 1941 J.E. CRADOCK-WATSON. (left April 1941) Scholarship at Wellington College.
Mar 1942 S.D.P. CLOUGH, 1st Scholarship at Harrow.
June 1942 E.W. FARGUS, 1st Scholarship at Oundle.
June 1942 A.N. WHARAM, 1st Scholarship at Denstone.
June 1944 C.N. RICHARDSON, 1st on Winchester Election Roll.
June 1944 K.A.C. PATTESON, 5th Open Scholarship at Marborough.
June 1944 K.A.C. PATTESON, 2nd Foundation Scholarship at Marlborough.
June 1944 C.B. ZEALLEY, 10th Scholarship at Sherborne.
June 1945 O.C. LEIGH-WILLIAMS, 6th on Winchester Election Roll.
June 1945 J.M. SHARMAN, 9th Scholarship at Rugby.
Nov 1945 T.L. CRUMBY, (left April 1945) Exhibition at Wellington College.

May 1946   T.G. WHITWORTH, 5th Foundation Scholarship at Marlborough.
June 1946   J.E.C. MACRAE, 5th Scholarship at Fettes.
June 1946   C.D. ROBINSON, Major Scholarship at Rugby.
June 1946   I.H.C. CORY, (left April 1945) Exhibition at Repton.
June 1947   I.H. GRIEG, Exhibition at Shrewsbury.
June 1947   P. DE N. LUCAS, 16th on Winchester Election Roll.
June 1947   M.G. BODDY, 11th Foundation Scholarship at Marlborough.
June 1947   R.B.B. RUMNEY, 3rd Scholarship at St. John's, Leatherhead.
May 1948   G.F. PARSONS, 1st Foundation Scholarship at Marlborough.
June 1948   G.F. PARSONS, 5th Open Scholarship at Marlborough.
June 1948   A.K. ZEALLEY, Exhibition at Sherborne.
June 1949   R.H. ROBINSON, 1st Scholarship at Uppingham.
June 1949   D.F. MANNING, 3rd Scholarship at Uppingham.
June 1949   D. SANDYS-RENTON, 1st Scholarship at Sherborne.
June 1949   R.A.W. GLEADOW, Major Scholarship at Oundle.
June 1949   R.W. WILKINSON, 1st Foundation Scholarship at Marlborough.
May 1950   J.B. WHITWELL, Exhibition at Bryanston.
June 1950   J.G. PARSONS, 1st Scholarship at Marlborough.
June 1950   W.O.F. WALLIS, 2nd Scholarship at Marlborough.
June 1950   W. WARE, 3rd on Winchester Election Roll.
June 1950   A.J. MERER, 8th on Winchester Election Roll.
June 1950   P.M. HUTCHINSON, Top Scholar at Sedbergh.
June 1951   T.W. BREWIS, (left 1950), 18th on Eton Election Roll.
June 1951   C.D. JAY, 2nd Scholarship at St. John's, Leatherhead.
May 1952   A.L. WALLIS, 1st Foundation Scholarship at Marlborough.
May 1952   R.S. BREWIS, 17th on Eton Election Roll.
June 1952   A.Q. GOGGS, 4th Open Scholarship at Shrewsbury.
June 1952   A.C. TAUSSIG, 3rd on Winchester Election Roll.
June 1952   M.E. PONSONBY, 13th on Winchester Election Roll.
June 1952   J.R. RAIMES, 15th on Winchester Election Roll.
May 1953   T.E.H. SABBEN-CLARE, Foundation Scholarship at St. Peter's, York.
May 1953   J.M. ELLISON, Exhibition at Repton.
May 1954   A.B. COULTASS, 9th Open Scholarship at Marlborough.
June 1954   J.P. SABBEN-CLARE, 1st on Winchester Election Roll.
June 1954   A.R.H. URQUHART, 1st Scholarship at Repton.
June 1954   H.W. PAYNE, Exhibition at Shrewsbury.
June 1954   J.R. WILD, Exhibition at Sedbergh.
May 1955   H.W. PAYNE, (left 1954) Charles Grundy Scholarship at Shrewsbury.
June 1955   J.A. ROBERTSON, Major Scholarship at Oundle.
Mar 1956   J.R. ARCHER, Townsend-Warner History Prize (1st)
May 1956   J.R. ARCHER, 3rd Scholarship at Rugby.
June 1956   C.A.S. URQUHART, Major Scholarship at Repton.
June 1956   M.T. SYKES, Major Scholarship at Sedbergh.
June 1956   R.H. SYKES, 16th on Winchester Election Roll.

Mar 1957 H.W. PROSSER, 8th Scholarship at Harrow.

Mar 1957 A.J. TAUSSIG, Townsend-Warner History Prize (4th)

June 1957 R.E.J. WIGHTMAN, Exhibition at Uppingham.

June 1957 A.J. TAUSSIG, 3rd on Winchester Election Roll.

June 1957 A.F.J. HUNTER, Minor Scholarship at Oundle.

Mar 1958 S.R.J. FORD, Clergy Exhibition at Lancing.

June 1958 D.C. ROYLE, 13th on Winchester Election Roll.

June 1958 R.E.J. WIGHTMAN, (left 1957) Exhibition at Uppingham.

May 1959 S.W. PAYNE, Exhibition at Shrewsbury.

May 1959 J.R. CARR, (left December 1958) Exhibition at Repton.

June 1959 P.K. WINGFIELD DIGBY, 2nd Foundation Scholarship at Marlborough.

May 1960 W.M. WRIGLEY, 4th Queen's Scholarship at Winchester.

June 1960 S.W. PAYNE, (left 1959) 3rd Open Scholarship at Shrewsbury.

June 1960 G.K. CHARLTON, Exhibition at Fettes.

June 1960 N.C. BRADFORD, (left 1959) Exhibition at Fettes.

June 1960 D.J. MACKELLAR, Exhibition at Sedbergh.

Mar 1961 E.J. PYBUS, Exhibition at Lancing.

June 1961 G.K. CHARLTON, (left 1960) Exhibition at Fettes.

May 1962 I.W. LITTLEWOOD, Barclay's Bank Educational Scheme Open Scholarship at St. Edward's, Oxford.

June 1962 H.C.F. BOWRING, 1st Scholarship at Marlborough.

June 1962 C.G. TREASURE, Open Scholarship at Shrewsbury.

June 1962 I.R. MACKELLAR, Minor Scholarship at Sedbergh.

May 1963 F.R.M. BREWIS, (left July 1962) 7th on Eton Election Roll.

May 1963 I.W. LITTLEWOOD, (left July 1962) Major Open Scholarship at St. Edward's.

May 1963 C.E. WATERHOUSE, Minor Scholarship at Uppingham.

May 1963 J.C.T. WEBSTER, (left March 1963) Major Scholarship at Sedbergh.

May 1963 G.G. WRIGLEY, Clergy Exhibition at Uppingham.

May 1964 A.N. DRAKE, Exhibition at The Leys.

June 1964 C.E. WATERHOUSE, (left July 1963) 3rd Open Scholarship at Uppingham.

May 1965 A.S. TREASURE, (left December 1964) Minor Scholarship at Shrewsbury.

May 1965 J.M. PARK, 9th on Winchester Election Roll.

June 1967 W.J. ROGERS, Minor Scholarship at Sedbergh.

June 1967 A.S.N. SMITH, Exhibition at Uppingham.

June 1967 S.J. WRIGLEY, (left March 1967) Clergy Exhibition at Uppingham.

June 1967 J.V. WRIGHT, (left July 1966) 1st Scholarship at Charterhouse.

May 1968 F.S. TREASURE, Minor Scholarship at Shrewsbury.

May 1969 H.E.V. ROSS, (left July 1968) 5th on Winchester Election Roll.

May 1969 J.B. CROOKS, 4th Scholarship at Uppingham.

May 1970 A.T. CAREY, 3rd Major Scholarship at Malvern.

Mar 1971 M.O. STONEHOUSE, Townsend-Warner History Prize (10th)

May 1971   M.W. WILLIAMS, 17th on Winchester Election Roll.
May 1971   J.J. ROGERS, Major Exhibition at Sedbergh.
May 1973   J.M. STONEHOUSE, 4th Scholarship at Uppingham.
May 1973   J.N. BARNARD, 1st Music Scholarship at Stowe.
Mar 1974   R.C.W. TODD, Townsend-Warner History Prize (14th)
May 1974   D.P. ROBINSON, 5th Scholarship at Rugby.
May 1974   W.R. THOMAS, 1st Scholarship at Worksop.
May 1974   R.C.W. TODD, 1st Scholarship at Sedbergh.
May 1974   T.M.C. MANSEL, 17th on Winchester Election Roll.
Mar 1975   J.R. WARE, Townsend-Warner History Prize (8th).
Mar 1975   A.K.F. PEASE, 5th Scholarship at Harrow.
Mar 1975   R.C.B. HENSON, 3rd Scholarship at Radley.
Mar 1976   M.O. POPE, Exhibition at Radley.
Mar 1976   M.B. WEST-TAYLOR, Top Scholarship at Pocklington.
Mar 1976   J.R. WARE, Townsend-Warner History Prize (2nd).
Mar 1976   J.R. WARE, 16th on Winchester Election Roll.
Mar 1977   A.M. TODD, Music Scholarship at Malvern.
Mar 1977   R.F. ROTHWELL, 1st Scholarship at Felsted.
Mar 1977   J.H.C. LORD, 12th Scholarship at Shrewsbury.
May 1977   W.H. HEPPELL, 1st Scholarship at Ampleforth.
May 1977   R.A.O. TODD, Exhibition at Sedbergh.
Mar 1978   J.H.C. LORD, 3rd Scholarship at Shrewsbury.
Mar 1978   G.J.G. BASTABLE, 14th Scholarship at Rugby.
Mar 1978   M.N. BASS, Exhibition at Durham.
May 1978   J.W. APPLEYARD, 2nd Scholarship at Ampleforth.
Apr 1979   W.D. PEEL-YATES, 1st Scholarship at Harrow.
Apr 1979   M.T. ALBAN, Music Scholarship at Sedbergh.
May 1979   W.J.B. WARD, Exhibition at Oundle.
May 1979   G.W.B TODD, 1st Scholarship at Sedbergh.
May 1979   M.T. ALBAN, Exhibition at Sedbergh.
May 1979   R. FULLER-SESSIONS, Scholarship at Queen Margaret's, Esc-
           rick.
Mar 1980   P.E.O. POCOCK, Exhibition at Harrow.
Mar 1980   D.M. GERRARD, Scholarship at St. Anne's.
Mar 1980   M.G. APPLEYARD, Music Scholarship at Ampleforth.
Mar 1980   E.J. BAKER-CRESSWELL, Batsford Townsend-Warner History
           Prize (7th)
May 1980   W.J.B. WARD, 5th Scholarship at Oundle.
Mar 1981   J.T.C. LORD, 2nd Scholarship at Shrewsbury.
Mar 1981   N.A.J. HALL, 6th Scholarship at Harrow.
Mar 1981   R.W.J. HOLLINGBERY, The Thompson Scholarship at Radley.
Mar 1981   T.H. LEY Batsford Townsend-Warner History Prize (15th).
May 1981   T.J. WOOD, Exhibition at Uppingham.
May 1981   T.H. LEY, 1st (Grocers) Scholarship at Oundle.
Feb 1982   D.A.F. PEARSON, 1st Music Scholarship at Harrow.
Mar 1982   H.S.C. BREESE, 1st Scholarship at Glenalmond.
Mar 1982   S. FULLER-SESSIONS, 1st Scholarship at Abbotsholme.

Mar 1982   N.A.J. HALL, (left 1981) 1st Scholarship at Harrow.
May 1982   T.J. WOOD, (left 1981) Exhibition at Uppingham.
May 1982   I.A. GERRARD, Exhibition at Worksop.
May 1982   A. CANNON-BROOKES, Exhibition at Oundle.
May 1982   S.G.C. STOCKEN, 7th on Winchester Election Roll.
May 1982   R. BAKER-CRESSWELL, 16th on Winchester Election Roll.
June 1982   J.S. VERRIER, Exhibition at Giggleswick.
May 1983   I.A. GERRARD, 2nd Scholarship, at Worksop (left 82).
May 1983   A.J. WOODS, 2nd Scholarship at Uppingham.
May 1983   H.G.J. STEVENS, 1st Scholarship at Marlborough.
Mar 1984   M.E.J. HALL, Shepherd-Churchill Scholarship at Harrow.
Mar 1985   M.J.S. BOOTH, Music Scholarship at Sedbergh.
Mar 1985   M.J.S. BOOTH, Hart Scholarship at Sedbergh.
Mar 1985   D.H. DEWAR, Bruce Kinnoch Scholarship at Glenalmond.
May 1985   N.J. VERRIER, 2nd Scholarship at Giggleswick.
July 1986   A. BHOOMKAR, Sir Charles Wheeler Merit Award for Art.
Feb 1987   N.F.B. FULLER-SESSIONS, Minor Scholarship at Radley.
Mar 1987   D.J. DEWAR, Major Scholarship at Glenalmond.
May 1987   S.A. MARR, Major Scholarship at Stowe.
May 1987   R.H. PROCOPÉ, Major Scholarship at Rugby.
May 1987   P.S.J. COVILLE, Scholarship at Oundle.
Feb 1988   A.H.S. BOOTH, Music Scholarship at Sedbergh.
Feb 1988   A.H.S. BOOTH, 1st Scholarship at Sedbergh.
May 1988   A.M.S. HAND, 18th on Winchester Election Roll.
July 1988   D.R. MACKINNON, Sir Charles Wheeler Merit Award for Art.
May 1989   N.H. JONES, 2nd Equal Scholarship at Uppingham.
May 1989   C.W.G. DREYER, 4th on Winchester Election Roll.
May 1989   M.G.P. MATTHEWS, Continuation Scholarship at Repton.
May 1989   C.C. PROCOPÉ, 2nd Equal Scholarship at Rugby.
Feb 1990   J.D.C. KEALY, Music Scholarship at Uppingham.
Feb 1990   A.T. BIRLEY, Music Exhibition at Uppingham.
May 1990   M.J.W. DALLAS, 2nd Scholarship at Uppingham.
May 1990   M.G.P. MATTHEWS, Minor Scholarship at Repton.
Mar 1991   D.W. NICHOLSON, 6th Scholarship at Radley.
May 1991   G.R. MARKHAM, 2nd on Winchester Election Roll.
May 1991   A.D.A. HUNTER SMART, Exhibition at Uppingham.
May 1991   H.M. PROCOPÉ, 4th Scholarship at Rugby.
May 1991   O.L.H. HALLAM, 5th Scholarship at Oundle.
June 1991   G.R. BEAUMONT, Scholarship at Scarborough College.
Feb 1993   C.M. ABLETT, Music Exhibition at Repton.
Mar 1993   H.B. WHITTEN, Music Exhibition at Sedbergh.
May 1993   J.H.A. SUMMERFIELD, 19th on Winchester Election Roll.
May 1993   R.J. WILLIAMSON, 4th Scholarship at Uppingham.

In the last 10 years (1983-1992) boys have gone to the following public schools.

Uppingham	38	Ampleforth	7
Sedbergh	27	Stowe	7
Oundle	24	Glenalmond	4
Eton	18	St. Edward's	3
Radley	17	Marlborough	2
Harrow	17	Worksop	2
Shrewsbury	14	Loretto	2
Repton	13	St. Peter's, York	2
Rugby	12	Wellington College	2
Winchester	12	Scarborough College	2

In addition 1 boy in each case has gone to.

Bradfield	Giggleswick	Malvern
Cheltenham	Cokethorpe	Aldenham
The Leys	Ellesmere	Pocklington
Rannoch	St. David's	Hymers
Gordonstoun	Oakham	

INDEX

The initials of female staff were not recorded in the School Register for many years.